THE PERILS OF DEMOCRACY

OTHER BOOKS BY HERBERT AGAR

A Time for Greatness
The Unquiet Years: U.S.A. 1945–1955
The Saving Remnant
The United States:
The Presidents, the Parties and the Constitution
The People's Choice
(Pulitzer Prize)
Abraham Lincoln
Declaration of Faith
Pursuit of Happiness
(*The Story of American Democracy*)
Milton and Plato

The
Perils of Democracy

A BACKGROUND BOOK

Herbert Agar

© Herbert Agar 1965

CAPRICORN BOOKS EDITION 1968
Published by arrangement with
DUFOUR EDITIONS
Chester Springs, Pa.

PRINTED IN THE UNITED STATES OF AMERICA

CONTENTS

Preface, 7
1. Freedom, 9
2. Representative Democracy, 41
3. The New Nations, 77
   Index, 93

For
BARBIE

*The world will never be safe for democracy;
it is a dangerous trade.*

G. K. Chesterton

PREFACE

THE PERILS of democracy in practice are many. So are the perils of democracy in definition. Even in the West where we think we use the word rationally, few people give it the same meaning. And many people give it no meaning at all. They use it as a talisman, or charm, which if worn conspicuously will make them better citizens. Vain hope, for the charm is useless until its intricate workings are understood.

Therefore, in order to show the pitfalls of our system, and to suggest that with good will and common sense they might be evaded, I have tried to explain exactly what I mean by this many-coloured word, democracy. No matter how inadequate my definitions, if they are unequivocal they may still have relevance. At least we shall know what we are talking about.

I have tried to avoid the smug suggestion that our Western systems of government are the best or the only forms of democracy. Subtler and more successful ways of promoting freedom may be found by wiser people. But whatever the mechanics, the heart of the matter will be the same: a government which can be opposed without hatred and changed without violence and which seeks to promote whatever the citizens, helped by the wisest leaders they can find, consider to be their own and the world's best interests.

I owe a debt to Professor Sir Karl Popper whose book, *The Open Society and Its Enemies*, has taught me the danger of confusing history with prophecy and also some of the merits of Marx.

April, 1965
Beechwood
Petworth, Sussex

Herbert Agar

I
Freedom

In 1942, before the turn of the tide in the Second World War, a far-sighted Frenchman wrote: 'The real opposition to Hitler is not to be found either in Bolshevism, capitalism, socialism, or in the Jews. There is only one real peril for Hitler: democracy, and the principles upon which it is founded. If he can destroy that, he destroys all the rest. This word—so derided by some today, so meaningless to others—contains nevertheless the essential idea of continuity and evolution, of progress and permanence, without which there can be no civilisation.'*

The word democracy is not derided today; but it is in danger of becoming meaningless since every nation claims to be a democracy of sorts and since all the claims cannot possibly be true. We have 'people's democracy', 'basic democracy', 'participating democracy' and just plain democracy as we understand it in the West. We also have dictatorships which call themselves democracies in order to qualify for American aid. Almost every nation on earth today would claim to be a democracy in one of those senses. Yet in 1942, when Roussy de Sales wrote, our numerous enemies who had conquered half the globe were united in thinking democracy decadent and outmoded. Nothing succeeds like success.

Amid this welter of 'democracies' we should try to be precise on two points: first, what the word means to us in the light of our Western experience; second, what aspects of democracy are essential and universal, as opposed to those which are the product of our own environment and way of life. If we can answer the second question we may have much of interest to offer the new nations, and vice versa.

The 'Third World' is irritated when we say it should have

* Raoul de Roussy de Sales, *The Making of Tomorrow*.

an exact copy of the parliamentary or presidential system, complete with two chambers, etc. Its problems are incommensurate with ours, so it doubts whether it can swallow our solutions whole. Yet all men want freedom if they can find it. And democratic government is nothing but a device to organise the most freedom possible, and to maintain it. The latter is the more difficult, as the new countries are already finding. So if we can describe the many dangers which are inherent in our form of democracy, why it can never attain security or a state of equilibrium, how difficult and elusive it is—how hard to preserve when you have it and how desperately hard to create when you have it not—and why it has to be defended all over again all the time, we may be of some use to our newborn neighbours. And if we look closely at their tremendous problems, and at how they are struggling with them, we may learn something of use to us. Government is a very rough affair and can never be satisfactory, but that is no reason why it should not be improved.

In our search for definition we must begin with the so-called 'pure' democracy of ancient Athens, wherein every citizen was a legislator and was responsible for electing the generals and choosing the magistrates by lot. This system sounds less 'pure' when we remember that ninety per cent of the residents were slaves or foreigners or women and thus took no part in public life.

Yet the Athenian democracy has been decisive for the Western world in two ways: first, it taught us the meaning of freedom, of individualism, of relying upon our own powers of reason and criticism, thus inspiring us to deny the right of tyrants, autocracies, totalitarian states, to tell us what to do. Whether we are conscious of it or not, our never-ending resistance against the eternally renascent tyrant-state is made in defence of the ideas first preached by such men as Pericles, Socrates and Democritus the Thracian. And second, the Athenian democracy in day-to-day practice helped to teach us what not to do, how to protect ourselves from the worst faults of free men.

Let us speak first of the glorious side. 'Although only a few may originate a policy,' said Pericles in his famous funeral oration, 'we are all able to judge it.' This is the affirmation on which democracy rests. We can all argue, criticise, join with our friends in attacking or promoting a policy. Thus we can all be responsible. We can all be citizens. The future depends on how we behave, not on an historian's apocalyptic visions and not on a tyrant's whims. We become what we do. So does the world we live in, if enough of us do it—whether 'it' be good or detestable. This is the burden of freedom: that it is all our fault, or our credit, and that we can never blame fate. This is what a few Athenians, plus a few foreigners in Athens, taught for the first time in the fifth century B.C. We are still trying—sometimes, it seems, against all hope—to make their words come true.

In the same oration, as reported by Thucydides (a man of the Right who distrusted democracy), Pericles said: 'Our constitution is named a democracy because it is in the hands not of the few but of the many. But our laws secure equal justice for all in their private disputes.... And as we give free play to all in our public life, so we carry the same spirit into our daily relations with one another. We have no black looks or angry words for our neighbour if he enjoys himself in his own way.... Yet ours is no work-a-day city. No other provides so many recreations for the spirit—contests and sacrifices all year round, and beauty in our public buildings to cheer the heart and delight the eye day by day.... We are lovers of beauty without extravagance, and lovers of wisdom without unmanliness.... Our citizens attend both to public and private duties, and we do not allow absorption in their own various affairs to interfere with their knowledge of the city's. We consider the man who holds aloof from public life not as harmless but as useless.... Such were the men who lie here, and such the city that inspired them.... The whole earth is the sepulchre of famous men; and their story is not graven only on stone over their native earth, but lives on far away, without visible symbol, woven into the stuff of other men's lives.'

All this, as we shall see, was too good to be true. But the speech was directed to the entire population of Athens, to celebrate the memory of the dead in the first year of the Peloponnesian War. The exaggerations may be forgiven. They show us the ideas and the hopes which were then in the air, hopes which are woven into the stuff of our own lives and which in that sense preserve the memory of those dead men.

When Socrates was on trial for his life, on the charge of being impious (which he was, like all men who insist on thinking for themselves), he told the court: 'I am the gadfly that God has attached to this city, and all day long and in all places I am fastening upon you, arousing and persuading and reproaching you. You would not readily find another like me, and therefore I should advise you to spare me.... If you rashly put me to death, then you will remain asleep for the rest of your lives, unless God in his care sends you another gadfly.'

Later, after the death-sentence, he returns to this theme: 'I say that this is the greatest good to man, to discourse daily on virtue, and on other things which you have heard me discussing, examining both myself and others, for the unexamined life is not worth living.... You have done this (i.e., condemned Socrates to death) thinking you would be freed from the necessity of giving an account of your life.'

The gadfly and the examined life, these are essential for democracy. Nothing is allowed to pass without criticism. Nothing is accepted because important people say it is true. Only after long argument is a policy adopted. Such freedom is a hard taskmaster. Men grow weary and abandon it. Then they grow lonely and seek it again.

We should not wonder that the Athenians put Socrates to death. He belonged to the first generation in Western history which asserted the absolute right to free thought, free criticism and freedom to cast doubt on all men's most intimate prejudices. Since we still persecute our gadflies today, we should be surprised that the first of this long line of mind-adventurers lived to be seventy.*

Turning from the inspiration of these great men to the mundane democracy of Athens, we find a sad decline and also a lesson in how not to run a free society. Thucydides and Plato and Aristotle may all have been prejudiced in their picture of Athens. The first two certainly belonged to the anti-democratic party. Yet allowing for exaggeration, they unite in giving us a picture of reckless inconsequence.

By the time of the Peloponnesian War (431–404 B.C.), all power in Athens was in the hands of the popular assembly—the adult male citizens of whom there were some forty thousand in Periclean Athens. This unwieldy lump, or such parts of it as chose to make the most trouble, had the power to suspend magistrates and bring them to trial. Thus the executive merely carried out the orders of 'the people'. The once-powerful Council of Five Hundred had lost control and could merely discuss policies which the assembly could accept, or change, or reject. Law was in the hands of a judicial assembly of six thousand members, chosen by lot. In groups of five hundred or more, these 'judges', or 'juries', or 'courts', or whatever they were, heard all cases. The magistrates presented the cases but took no further part. The verdict was given by a simple majority of votes.

From 443 until his death in 429, Pericles was the unchallenged leader of this odd government. He was re-elected general each year and his words carried weight with the un-

* We may ignore the endless argument about how to reconcile the Socrates of the *Apology* (quoted above) with the totalitarian Socrates of the *Republic*. Since Plato wrote both dialogues after the death of his master, one way to reconcile them is to assume that in the *Apology* and the *Crito* he was quoting the real Socrates whereas in the *Republic* he was putting his own ideas into the great man's mouth. For our purposes it does not matter. The words once spoken, or written, could never be recalled. It is the Socrates of the *Apology* and the *Crito* who has inspired democratic man from the beginning.

ruly assembly, but not enough weight to impose reason upon their inveterate turbulence. Meanwhile he made Athens most beautiful, hoping thereby to elevate the spirits of all the residents, free and slave alike. And her poets made Athens one of the wonders of the world. But her 'pure' democracy, which liberated men's energies for good, also liberated them for extreme evil and for self-destruction, making Athens hated throughout the eastern Mediterranean. She treated her allies like servile provinces and became known as the 'tyrant city'. As her trade with the Western Mediterranean grew important, her pride and her selfishness became intolerable. Her late allies, now her resentful subjects, turned for aid to Sparta.

The resulting Peloponnesian War was more than a struggle for empire between Athens and Sparta. Thucydides tells us that at the beginning of the war 'the whole Hellenic world was in commotion; in every city the chiefs of the democracy and of the oligarchy were struggling, the one to bring in the Athenians, the other the Lacedaemonians'. Strangely, the same was true within Athens herself. In the midst of the war, adventurers such as Alcibiades, and leaders of the oligarchic party such as Critias, were constantly conspiring with Sparta. Yet when the war had been lost, largely because of this treason, Alcibiades was invited to return to Athens because his high abilities were needed. One must assume that to the Greeks of the fifth century B.C. treason was a legitimate form of politics.

Had Pericles not died of the plague in the third year of the war, the Athenian democracy might have behaved better; but in fact it gave a sad display of rashness and cruelty. When the war was as good as won, in 415, the assembly allowed Alcibiades to tempt it to extend the Athenian conquests into Sicily, and then failed to back Alcibiades with all its might. The result was a defeat so disastrous that the oppressed 'allies' revolted and thenceforth there was no real hope.

Before her defeat, however, Athens gave an impressive

warning of the cruelty which is latent in a democracy. 'The people', left to themselves, unprotected by wise and time-honoured institutions, can become a frightened and thus a bloodthirsty mob.

In the sixteenth year of the Peloponnesian War, Athens invaded the small island of Melos, a protectorate of Sparta but hitherto neutral in the war. In a popular frenzy, which had no political or military meaning, the Athenians demanded that Melos renounce Sparta and become an ally, which meant a semi-slave. Thucydides recreates the dialogue between the Athenian envoys and the Melians. Except for the absence of ranting, it could be a dialogue between Hitler and any of his helpless victims. For example:

> *Athenians*: 'You know, and we know, as practical men, that the questions of justice arise only between parties equal in strength, and that the strong do what they can, and the weak submit.... We wish you to become our subjects with the least trouble to ourselves, and we would like you to survive in our interests as well as your own....'
>
> *Melians*: 'Would you not agree to an arrangement under which we should keep out of war, and be your friends instead of your enemies?'
>
> *Athenians*: 'No.... We believe that Heaven, and we know that men, by a natural law, always rule where they are stronger.... As to your expectations from Lacedaemon and your belief that she will help you from a sense of honour, we congratulate you on your innocence but we do not admire your folly.'

Nevertheless the Melians put their trust in Sparta, and resisted. Their ancient and beautiful capital city was quickly overcome. Sparta gave no aid. The democratic assembly at Athens, on the motion of Alcibiades, decreed that all the grown men of Melos should be killed and that all the women and children should be sold into slavery. Subsequently the Athenians sent out five hundred settlers to colonise the island.

Winston Churchill might have had the fate of Melos in mind when he said, during his first years in Parliament, 'Democracy is more vindictive than Cabinets. The wars of peoples will be more terrible than those of kings.' That was in 1901, thirteen years before the first of the 'wars of peoples' which have almost brought our society to its knees.

Plato was born in the third year of the Peloponnesian War, which may explain why he felt that democracy is the disorderly parent of tyranny, and liberty the parent of slavery. 'Tyranny', he wrote, 'is established out of no other form than democracy—and out of the highest degree of liberty, methinks, comes the greatest and fiercest slavery.'

We should remember that Plato was writing about a government by plebiscite wherein the fleeting will of the majority—inhibited by no Constitution and responsible to no courts—was sovereign and supreme. This interpretation of democracy has normally led to the totalitarian state. Any day, any hour, the people can do exactly what they want; so the power of the tyrant becomes legitimate since it was handed to him by a bewitched majority. This is how Napoleon III made himself Emperor and how Hitler made himself demigod. As the result of one election in 1933, Hitler hoped to establish the Nazis for a thousand years. In other words, the people are so supreme that they can vote themselves into slavery. This is an obvious hazard of popular government. No system can save the people from an enduring folly, but the more sober democracies of the West have at least devised means to save them from a sudden hysteria.

Aristotle, who was born nineteen years after the Peloponnesian War, and who did not see the wildest excesses of the Athenian assembly in its days of fright and defeat, took a more temperate view of democracy, but scarcely a more friendly one. He believed, reasonably enough on the basis of his Greek experience, that it cannot maintain the golden mean, that it tends always to the extreme and thus to a breakdown into anarchy. Yet he admitted that if democracy could be made the servant of the law, could accept the sovereignty of the law, it might become a blessing. The moment we think in terms of the supremacy of law we leave the ill-fated Greek democracies and turn to the modern concept of constitutional government.

Before dismissing the Greeks, we should remind ourselves that the large majority of Athenians proved many times that they preferred their democracy (defeats, disorders, cruelties and all) to any other form of government. They fought to get it and they fought to keep it and they fought to restore it when Sparta imposed an oligarchy after the Peloponnesian War. The oligarchs, known as 'the Thirty', included Plato's cousin and his uncle. They treated their native city like booty of war. For eighteen months it was the reign of murder and plunder—a Terror far worse than that of the French Revolution—until the democrats killed the leaders of the Thirty and restored their old constitution. One wishes they had not denigrated their victory by putting Socrates to death; but his friendship with Plato and Plato's relatives must have stood him in bad stead. On the whole, the renewed democrats behaved better than the old, perhaps because the temptations were less since Athens's fall from power. For almost three generations the democracy continued until extinguished by Philip of Macedon at Chaeronea in 338.

2

A very old nation may sidle its way during centuries toward constitutional government. A very young nation, setting up house for the first time, must define its purpose with care and use all its willpower to serve that purpose and not to slump into a random chaos. This may be why the leaders of the United States, in 1787, set themselves to invent a written constitution, while the British evolved an unwritten one over some eight centuries of trial and error.

The Americans who met in Philadelphia to discuss their document were the heirs to a century and a half of agitated thinking, in England and France, about the nature of government. They were also the heirs to the experience and the theories of the classical world. They had studied the medieval free cities of Italy, whose histories seemed to confirm the Platonic diagnosis of oligarchy into democracy into tyranny. And they were wise men. Their debates, and their subsequent defence of their newly-devised system, are of interest to any nation, starting afresh, which is trying to find its way toward freedom and constitutionalism.

The men of Philadelphia did not talk much about democracy, and when they did it was usually in disparaging terms since their chief models were the Greeks. 'The ancient democracies', said Alexander Hamilton when speaking in defence of the Constitution, 'in which the people themselves deliberated, never possessed one feature of good government. Their very character was tyranny.'

The fathers of the American Republic concentrated their thoughts upon freedom. A few of them talked about equality; but most of them agreed with Goethe: 'Lawgivers or revolutionaries who promise equality and liberty at the same time are either utopian dreamers or charlatans.' Social democracy, however, was in the air in America (if we forget the slaves, as most men did). Social democracy was a fact of life on the frontier, which was then not far from the Atlantic seaboard. As democracy spread, and invaded the field of government, it had no trouble in adapting the Constitution to its usages. This is interesting: a constitution devised to protect freedom can absorb, and cherish, and become integral with an expanding political democracy. On the other hand, an egalitarian constitution, devised solely to implant democracy, might have gone the old sad route into tyranny for the government and slavery for the citizen.

So we may hazard one statement about democracy: it is a means toward an end, and the end is freedom. It is freedom which men have always wanted and upon which they must always insist, for without freedom human beings cannot become fully human. Henry Commager, the American historian, puts the case strongly: 'We must preserve and encourage the exercise of freedom of inquiry, investigation, dissent, association, education, science, literature, politics—freedom, in short, in all of its manifestations, not as an abstract right but as an imperative necessity.... We do not encourage dissent for sentimental reasons; we encourage dissent because we cannot live without it. The only enterprise that is really private is intellectual enterprise, and upon this depends all other enterprise.'

Although these thoughts are heretical in the Communist world, they are not a mere Western eccentricity. Pandit Nehru wrote: 'I do not see any real progress unless the individual progresses, and I do not see any individual progress unless a much larger measure of freedom is given to him.' And Charles Malik of the Lebanon, one-time President of the Assembly of the United Nations, agrees: 'It is only in free cultures, namely, in cultures where the first principle is not the state or the party or the nation or the system or some abstract philosophy, but the individual human person in all his dignity and possibility, that real equality and respect can flourish.' Here is the absolute. Constitutional democratic government is a piece of machinery for helping us towards this absolute. We criticise Greek democracy, not because it gave too much freedom but because, lacking safeguards, it tended to break down after brief excesses and give no freedom at all. Constitutional democracy is the best piece of machinery, for preserving freedom, which we know of today. We must therefore defend it. And we must try by our example to induce the new nations to experiment with it. But if we were to find another piece of machinery, which supported freedom better, we should be ready to jettison our own awkward devices.

In other words, we should treat political democracy as we should treat an economic system, asking only 'Is this the best support for the freedom of the individual?' When Khrushchev told us that he and his compatriots would bury us, he probably meant that before long the Soviet economic system would produce cheaper and better goods and services than the mixed economies of the West. He probably had in mind the immense effort towards automation which he had decreed and which he believed would in time put his country in advance of the West. In 1959 a Soviet economist made the interesting statement that 'If capitalism can be characterised as a classical period of the mechanisation of work, Communism will be seen to bring about a new era of total automation in production.'

This is all very well; but we must still ask the question, 'What about freedom in your automation-heaven?' The present strides towards automation in Russia are taken by edict and under compulsion. We of the West might be outstripped because we still choose to consult a great many people before turning an industry inside-out and moving most of the workers. In other words we still choose to remain as free as possible. Nevertheless, if the day should ever come when the question, 'What about freedom?', could be answered in Communist fact as it is answered in fancy by the prophets of Communism, if that system could produce not only more goods and services but more freedom, we would gladly bury our present clanking and half-efficient methods.

Heaven knows, democracy can also inhibit freedom. But it inhibits it less today than any other system. Winston Churchill put it accurately in the House of Commons in 1947: 'It has been said that democracy is the worst form of government except all those other forms that have been tried from time to time.'

Before searching further for a definition of democracy, let us look at the freedom, or freedoms, it is intended to preserve. In January 1941, Franklin Roosevelt spoke of four freedoms: freedom of speech and expression; freedom of worship; freedom from want; freedom from fear. The first two are our inheritance from the revolutions of the seventeenth and eighteenth centuries. The second two, if taken seriously, are even more revolutionary in their implications.

Freedom of speech and expression covers the whole field of communication, including the perilous mass media of today. It is a limited freedom because there must always be some things which people are not free to write or say. No one has a 'right', as Oliver Wendell Holmes put it, to yell 'fire' in a crowded theatre. Yet freedom of speech, which is a necessity for civilised and intellectual life, can also be a great danger to that life. We cannot do without it; but it can easily drag us down. It requires of the citizen a constant discipline (whether he be talking on a soap-box or editing a newspaper or running a television station) lest it become one of the greatest of the perils of democracy.

We all know that such discipline is not steadily exercised. The names of certain newspaper proprietors, or the unlamented name of the late Senator McCarthy, will remind us of how easily we fail in this duty—bad newspapers and bad senators being in part our own fault.

There is doubtless no solution to the problem of the press, since it is merely the problem of human nature writ large. Free, the press can do great harm, and often does; but it can also improve if the producers and the consumers improve. Muzzled, the press is a catastrophe and can undermine our hope of freedom.

The press must be left free because it can help us to keep an eye on government. But the press knows that most people would rather keep an eye on beauty queens and on the sexual habits of 'society'. How far can we blame the mass-circulation papers for acting on this knowledge? Perhaps the most we can hope for, and ask for, is that the irresponsible newspapers should be less sanctimonious. While feeding us 'vital statistics' and slanted news and unfair comment, they might at least refrain from telling us what a godsend they are and how deprived we should feel without them.

McCarthyism, also, is a disease from which we cannot wholly protect ourselves. The disease will recur whenever we become slack or frightened. The roots of McCarthyism were, first, the failure of American liberals during the 1930s to preserve the liberal faith when dealing with Stalinism, and second, the fears of too many people when confronted with such disagreeable facts as the conquest of China by Communism, the treachery of Fuchs and the seeming treachery of Hiss, and the Russian acquisition of the bomb.

Because the liberals had failed to grasp the nature of Stalinism during the 1930s, because in their horror at the great depression (and at the fat complacence of the Harding–Coolidge era) they had neglected freedom and half-defended the politics of slavery, they seemed vulnerable to the post-war accusation of crypto-Communism even when it came from a senatorial ruffian. And because the American people (like the British) had welcomed victory with the shallow hope that victory meant peace and that power could now be disbanded, they were shattered and unnerved when faced by a hostile China plus an aggressive Russia backed by a hundred divisions and the atom bomb. Someone must have betrayed them, else how could the rosy summer of 1945 have turned so dark so quickly? Thus the old slackness and the new fear combined to create a public for McCarthy. Such senators will always turn up, like dry rot in a neglected house, the moment the people are in a mood to suspend the vigilant defence of civil liberties.

Why did McCarthyism flourish in America, where civil liberties are guaranteed in detail by the so-called Bill of Rights which was appended to the Constitution in 1791, rather than in Britain where there are no such guarantees and where the temptations were similar (leftish flirtation with Stalinism in the 1930s; hasty demobilisation leaving the nation helpless before the Russians who had been aided by British traitors such as Fuchs)? The answer seems to be that civil liberties (a by-product of political liberty) are safer when that liberty is the result of a long experience and a slow evolution.

There is nothing in writing to prevent a British Government, with a workable majority in Parliament, from sweeping all civil liberties into the gutter. The Government does not do so, even in dangerous times, not because the act would be 'unconstitutional' but because the people would be displeased.

'Liberty,' writes Ivor Jennings, 'is the consequence of an attitude of mind rather than of precise rules.... The source of our liberty is not in laws or institutions, but in the spirit of free people.'

A long, long time is needed to evolve an unwritten Constitution which is protected only by 'an attitude of mind'. The United States did not have time, and neither will the new nations. But McCarthy should remind us all that no matter how carefully our 'rights' may be listed in a document they are worthless if the public abandons that 'spirit of free people' which alone protects liberty.

In the modern world, freedom of speech is also threatened in the name of 'security', which usually means the withholding of information. All very well to be allowed to say what you think, but suppose you are not allowed to think about a most important subject because the vital facts are denied you in the name of the 'national interest'?

'Security' can defeat itself in several ways. By withholding facts it can stifle imagination and criticism and the creative dissent which Professor Commager rightly says is essential. By preventing the old, free, international exchange among men of science, it may condemn many able thinkers to waste their years over problems which have already been solved or which have proved insoluble. And by an excess of hush-hush it may even provoke untimely revelations. A few weeks before the bomb fell on Hiroshima the author of this book, who was then connected with the American Embassy in London, made a speech at Clifton College, Bristol. Security was so great that he had not only not been told what was happening, he had not even been told not to talk about what might be happening. So in the course of the speech he remarked, in passing, that we were lucky the Germans had been defeated before they had developed the well-known possibilities of atomic energy.... A notable flare-up followed. Admirals were flown from Washington. Words like 'treason' were used. And all because of security.

Talleyrand pointed out that 'non-intervention' was merely

a long word for intervention. Perhaps 'security' is a short word for insecurity.

Rebecca West, in *The New Meaning of Treason*, deplores the stifling of the man of science but concludes that we can do nothing about it in our present half-deranged world: 'It is ridiculous to think of small groups of persons with rare gifts working on related facts of high importance to our species, at points dotted over the globe, and failing to pool their discoveries. But the universe is constantly forcing us to do ridiculous things for the sake of our survival.' And Dame Rebecca mentions another form of insecurity resulting from our world-wide overproduction of babies. 'Our fruitfulness', she writes, 'is the real foe of security.... We are threatened by collaboration between the primary form of over-population and its secondary form.... The vast population excretes a number of documents so vast that a vast number of people have to be employed to work on them, so vast that it becomes impossible to buy their honesty by high wages and impossible to employ enough security officers to see that they keep filing cupboards locked and take nothing secret home.'

'Security', in any form, is an enemy of freedom. We have to live with the enemy; but we should watch him always with a sturdy distrust, diminish his powers rapidly when possible, and increase those powers only under the heaviest pressure of danger. The powers should never be increased by executive order (since the more 'security' the less trouble for the executive), but only by legislation after public debate.

Mr Roosevelt's second freedom, that of worship, now means the opposite to what it meant among the Puritans who fled to America. They wanted freedom to worship in one way only, and freedom to see to it that nobody disagreed with them. Religious toleration, they said, 'firmly provides free stableroom and litter for all kinds of consciences, be they ever so dirty or jadish'. This was abominable to the men of Plymouth and Massachusetts Bay. But it was precisely what President Roosevelt wanted: that all over the world men should have consciences as 'jadish' as they chose.

In a world of declining religious conviction this is the easiest of the freedoms to support and it imposes the least discipline upon us. The one metaphysical belief to which most of us in the West still cling is that every individual is unique and that his personality should be left so far as possible to come to flower in its own way. 'Freedom is therefore a great good, tolerance a great virtue and regimentation a great misfortune.'* Yet this great virtue, tolerance, can also become a danger. Democracy, to survive, must find some political means of preventing the virtue from turning into poison.

Are we to extend the full toleration of our democracy to those who are bent on replacing constitutional government with tyranny? Since regimentation is a great misfortune, at what point do we tell those who are planning to regiment us to stop talking? At what point should the Weimar Republic have told the Nazis to stop? The Germans may be more adept at mass hysteria than most of us; but we are all subject to the same disease. Tyrants can deal with it by jailing or killing those who show the first signs of infection; but how do democrats protect themselves?

Walter Lippmann has called attention to another odd by-product of the freedom of worship; it places the churches in an anomalous position. 'Inwardly, to their communicants, they continue to assert that they possess the only complete version of the truth. But outwardly, in their civic relations with other churches and with the civil power, they preach and practise toleration.... It is difficult to remain warmly convinced that the authority of any one sect is divine, when as a matter of daily experience all sects have to be treated alike.' This is doubtless what the Puritans had in mind when they said that freedom meant the right to worship in *their* way, the *correct* way, and that all error was slavery.

One of the classical eighteenth-century freedoms which Franklin Roosevelt did not mention is the freedom of assembly. This is less important today than it was to our

* Aldous Huxley, *Brave New World Revisited*, p. 120.

ancestors because of our mechanical means of communication. Yet one cannot imagine a free society in which it was denied. And one can scarcely imagine a greater danger to freedom. Hitler has shown us for the thousandth time that when people are assembled in a crowd they can eagerly toss overboard their powers of reasoning and yield themselves to excesses of rage and fear and cruelty. A demagogue who knows how to play upon their crowd-intoxicated passions can persuade them of almost anything, including believing in Hitler. So here is one more necessity of civilised life which is a risk to civilisation.

Another freedom which has become essential in our society of high technology is the freedom of association. This means, above all, the freedom of wage-earners to form themselves into trade unions which are controlled by their members, or by their members in association with other unions. Such associations create a new type of property and help to solve one of the oldest problems of government: how can people without property be made genuinely free?

James Harrington in the seventeenth century (a Republican and also a friend of Charles I during the Civil War, who got into trouble with both sides) wrote a classic book on the relations between property and power.* Inevitably, writing in the seventeenth century, he meant mainly landed property. And the Americans, who sought to make a free man's Constitution a hundred and twenty-one years later and who were much influenced by Harrington's book, thought chiefly in terms of the small freehold, the blacksmith shop, the village store, the coastal sailing ship.

Putting aside the slaves (as all men seem to have done in all their thinking), how could citizens who owned none of these things be protected in their freedom? James Madison wrote in *The Federalist*,† when defending the draft Con-

* *The Commonwealth of Oceania*, 1656.

† *The Federalist* is a collection of essays written by Alexander Hamilton, James Madison and John Jay, in 1788, to promote the ratification of the Constitution of the United States.

stitution to the public which had not yet accepted it, 'Power over a man's support is power over his will.' John Adams compressed the seemingly undeniable truth into three words: 'Power follows property.'

The somewhat gingerly approach to democracy in the written Constitution of the United States is explained by this dilemma: if power follows property, how can we give political power to those who have no property? Are they not certain to become the dupes, or the henchmen, of those who control their livelihood? A few artists here and there, a few writers—they can do no harm. But what about the increasing number of men who work in other men's shops, inns, or on other men's land? No man can use his freedom of speech, or of worship, or of assembly, if he is in danger of losing his job should the boss disagree—unless he is a saint, and there is no need to legislate for saints. Those who are economically unfree are subject to blackmail. Is it wise to give political power to men who are subject to blackmail?

The answer could not be found at Philadelphia. Yet political democracy went forward. And it is interesting to note that in America it did so under pressure from the backcountry, from the ever-moving frontier, where practically every family did in fact own property. Within forty years of the acceptance of the Constitution, political democracy was to assert itself decisively in the person of President Andrew Jackson. But the total freedom of association, the unrestricted right to form trade unions (with the protection of the government as in the case of other forms of property), did not come in the United States until the days of Franklin Roosevelt and the New Deal. It came earlier in Great Britain, but there too it proved a difficult form of freedom to ensure. One reason for the difficulty is that freedom of association does truly create a new form of property or of power: the pooled power of the workers in an industry. And all forms of property are troublesome to regulate, for governments who seek to preserve freedom.

3

In his pamphlet, *The Challenge of Democracy*, John Strachey mentioned still another freedom which he called the rule of law. 'This is one of the oldest and simplest freedoms,' he wrote, 'but it has turned out to be one of the most precious. It has turned out that if and when governments infringe this freedom and start imprisoning, arresting, torturing and killing people at their own sweet will, without regard to the public laws of the community, every other kind of freedom becomes impossible.' And he adds that this is a modest freedom, since it is not a question of good laws or bad laws, but merely that there should be *some* laws which are definite and comprehensible, which are not over-ridden by the executive or altered retroactively by the legislature and which are administered by honest courts.

This last is an ingenious attempt to sidestep the ancient argument about the sanction of law. Is it mere power, or does it derive at least in part from eternal truths? In other words, is there such a thing as 'natural law'? No one can come to terms with any theory of government until he knows what he thinks about natural law. And no theory of democracy can rest on the notion that 'the rule of law' can just as well mean the rule of bad laws as of good ones. We know what free people do with bad laws, or laws which they consider bad. They break them: steadily, angrily, openly, until the laws are repealed. The Prohibition law in the United States was an example. If all laws were treated as the Americans treated the Volstead Act (which made the Eighteenth Amendment to the Constitution legally effective), we should soon be back to the anarchy which Plato predicted as the doom of all democracies, and from which, he insisted, they can only be rescued by tyranny.

The laws which free people uphold, and which they are prepared to die defending, are based on something more impressive than the transient whims of a few legislators who have been blackmailed by pressure groups into voting what they do not believe. American Prohibition deserves careful study by anyone who upholds 'the rule of law' or who worries about the dangers to democracy.

As far back as colonial days some people were complaining that Americans drank too much. From time to time, beginning with Maine in 1846, various states experimented with anti-drink laws. This harmed nobody, since wines and spirits could be brought in from neighbouring states. But in 1895 the Anti-Saloon League, which had been born two years before in Ohio, became a national organisation. Then the blackmail began. The League was run by high-minded idealists who were totally unscrupulous in politics. This combination of the Puritan and the thug (of Blifil and Black George as Lord Chatham complained on one occasion) is hard to beat.

The League devised the perfect balance-of-power system. In any district where a close contest was likely, the League had only to marshal a small group of fanatics and offer them *en masse* to the candidate of either major party who would promise to vote for Prohibition. Usually both candidates made the promise, since this had no effect on their personal habits.

By such methods, and with some help from the evangelical churches and from the ill-repute of many badly-run saloons, a majority in both Houses of Congress had been persuaded, by 1917, to pass an amendment to the Constitution prohibiting 'the manufacture, sale or transportation' of intoxicating beverages. Nothing was said about the 'purchase' of such beverages. So the buyer was safe, whatever might happen to his source of supply. Three-quarters of the state legislatures quickly ratified the amendment and in October, 1919, the Volstead Act provided for the enforcement at law and defined 'intoxicating beverages' as any drink containing as much as one half of one per cent of alcohol.

The result, as is well known, was corruption on a scale that had not previously been seen in a modern civilised nation. The police, the law, the federal and state enforcement units, the Congress of the United States and President Harding, all became objects of derision and cynicism and distaste. The law had been changed; the Constitution had been changed; but nobody had even tried to change the habits or the consciences of the American people—including the people who had passed the law and changed the Constitution. The sanctimonious blacklegs who had brought all this about were so simple as to think that a law becomes a law because a lot of legislators have been pressured into voting for it.

The same problem—what is a law?—arises from the laws on sex in many modern countries. Here again the United States provides the extreme example. This has little to do with the federal government; but there is scarcely anything that is not forbidden in one or more of the states. And judging by the Kinsey reports there is nothing at all that is not done.

So when is a law a law? This is a key question for free men. Hobbes, who did not believe in the possibility, or even the desirability, of free men, said, 'It is not wisdom but authority that makes a law'. The state, he thought, could make people believe in anything it chose to enact, for 'the common people's minds are like clean paper, fit to receive whatsoever by Public Authority shall be printed upon them'. And Oliver Wendell Holmes, Justice of the Supreme Court of the United States, seemed to agree when in a petulant mood he wrote: 'As long as law means force—(and when it means anything else I don't care who makes it and will do as I damn please)—force means an army.' This is clearly inadequate. The United States had some two and a half million well-armed soldiers when the eighteenth (the Prohibition) amendment was ratified. No one suggested using the soldiers, as they returned from France, to enforce the amendment—because everyone know they wouldn't and couldn't. And today no one calls on the state militia to enforce the multitude of strange enactments about 'unnatural' practices or positions in bed—for the same reason. So there must be more to a law than Hobbes's 'authority' or Holmes's 'army'.

Sir Frederick Pollock was more helpful when he wrote: 'Law, on the whole, expresses the common conscience of those who are subject to it. If it did not, it would not be obeyed, at least in a free country.' But Sir Frederick believed in natural law, in its non-theological sense. 'If you mean to imply', he wrote to Holmes in 1918, 'that no one can accept natural law (= natural justice = reason as understood in the Common Law) without maintaining it as a body of rules known to be absolutely true, I do not agree.... If you deny that any principles of conduct are common to and admitted by all men who try to behave reasonably—well, I don't see how you can have any ethics or any ethical background for law.' If for Sir Frederick's 'all men' we were to substitute 'all men within our Western tradition' we might have the irreducible minimum of agreement on the sanction of law (serious law, not traffic acts, etc.) which is needed for a free society. Also the most modest and least controversial statement of natural law.

Natural law provides one of the oldest arguments in history, and one may say that even if it does not exist it has been of profound importance because so many people have believed in it. 'But for natural law', writes Professor d'Entrèves, 'the petty laws of a small peasant community of peninsular Italy would never have become the universal law of an international civilisation. But for natural law the great medieval synthesis of godly and of worldly wisdom would not have been possible. But for natural law there would probably have been no American and no French revolution, nor would the great ideals of freedom and equality have found their way into the law-books after having found it into the hearts of men.' This is all true. Furthermore, natural law has proved a strong ally in man's resistance to the tyrant state. But we still cannot prove that it exists, and it is as difficult to define as conscience.

The Hebrew prophets constantly proclaimed that true law was divine and thus paramount over kings and princes and established authorities; but the Greeks were the first to try to put this notion into mundane terms. Pericles, in his funeral oration, said that 'we (the Athenians) are also taught to observe those unwritten laws whose sanction lies only in the universal feeling of what is right'. And Democritus wrote: 'Not out of fear but out of a feeling of what is right should we abstain from doing wrong.' Sophocles had already written the *Antigone* wherein the heroine dies for refusing to obey a wicked law. Aristotle quotes *Antigone* in the first systematic attempt to explain natural law. 'There are two sorts of law,' he wrote, 'the particular and the universal. *Particular* law is the law defined and declared by each community for its own members.... *Universal* law is the law of nature.... There really exists, as all of us in some measure divine, a natural form of the just and unjust which is common to all men, even when there is no community or covenant to bind them to one another. It is this form which the Antigone of Sophocles' play evidently has in mind when she says that it was a just act to bury her brother Polynices in spite of Creon's decree to the contrary—just, she means, in the sense of being *naturally* just.' And he quotes Antigone trying to explain the 'law' which drives her to act:

> *'Not of today or yesterday its force:*
> *It springs eternal: no man knows its birth.'*

He also quotes Empedocles and Alcidamas as having similar beliefs. The idea was in the air and the Stoics carried it one step further. They said it was a law of nature that all men are born free and equal, bound to each other in charity. Such notions had small effect upon the slave-based Roman world; but they have been useful in modern revolutions.

They were useful, faintly useful, even to the Roman lawmakers, for the *Institutes* of Justinian state that 'the laws of nature... remain always stable and immutable, enacted as they are by the very Providence of God.' This seems to have meant no more than that the Justinian codes (Aristotle's *particular* law) should correspond as closely as possible to the *universal* law of nature. But if they didn't, there was still no remedy. Nevertheless, whether true or false, this admission that all laws should be judged by some standard of what men knew naturally to be right was an important bequest by the Empire to its many heirs.

In the Middle Ages this vague admission became a Christian dogma, expressed with stark and revolutionary lucidity by St Thomas Aquinas: 'All humanly enacted laws are in accord with reason to the extent that they derive from the natural law. And if a human law is at variance in any particular with the natural law, it is no longer legal, but rather a corruption of law.'

This did not mean, to the Middle Ages, that a man of his own volition could disobey accepted authority because he had decided that the authority was wrong, was contrary to the 'true' law. He had to wait until the Church decreed that a government, or a king, had acted 'at variance with the natural law'. Only then was he absolved from allegiance. But after the Reformation there was to be no more waiting, at least in the Protestant countries, for Mother Church to speak. Men like Milton decided for themselves whether the king was right or wrong, just or unjust. And so did Thomas Jefferson, and so did the makers of the French Revolution.

The old doctrine of natural law, which had justified rebellion to Antigone and the final authority of the Church to Aquinas, had become the chief enemy to absolutism by the eighteenth century. The sudden and startling success of the natural sciences brought this to pass. Just as Grotius in the seventeenth century claimed that the natural law, in regard to man's conduct, is built into the structure of the universe, can be discovered by pure reason and has no need for a supernatural sanction, so the men of science came to affirm that every phenomenon in nature is subject to a changeless law which man can uncover by the use of his faculties without the aid of divine revelation.

The justification of this daring thought came quickly in astronomy and physics, and men began to feel confident that they would one day know all the laws of the universe—including the laws of right conduct among men. One had only to read accurately in the book of nature, undeterred by superstition, to find these laws. There, in that book, John Locke discovered the eternal rightness of the Glorious Revolution of 1689. There Jefferson found that 'the Laws of Nature and of Nature's God' justified the Colonies' distaste for George III. And there the French found 'the Rights of Man and of the Citizen' in the name of which they upset their own government and conquered half of Europe.

We may say, therefore, that natural law has been of vast importance in history, since men believed in it; but we still do not know whether it really exists. It is wrapped in ambiguity and can be used by the enemies of freedom as well as by the friends. When used to justify a revolt against oppression we tend to salute it; but can we salute it when used to justify the oppression itself?

During the long wrangle over slavery in the United States, the abolitionists instinctively called upon the 'higher law', the law of nature, to discredit the Constitution and the laws of those states which permitted or imposed slavery. But the slave-holders appealed to the same 'book of nature' and found a different reading. Slavery was 'natural'; it was 'the result of some fixed law'. It was the necessary price of a high civilisation—a statement which could be justified by many quotations from the freedom-loving Greeks.

Perhaps the wisest course is to leave nature out of it, since we now know that nature is far more complicated and incomprehensible than the eighteenth century foresaw, and to leave God out of it, since we are too likely to believe that God is on our own side whatever side that may be. But we still need a sanction for a free man's law which is more acceptable than force. May we not find it in the humble sphere of human reason, or 'the common conscience of those who are subject to it'? Since we know that reason is unreliable and easily distorted by passion, we shall not be shocked or surprised when good men declare that slavery is reasonable, but we may hope that in the long run they may lose their argument.

The virtue of reason as a sanction is that the cause is never lost, whereas if we fall back upon the sword it may be lost in one engagement.

The Common Law of England (adopted in most of the United States) is an example of the mature application of reason. Starting with Saxon customs which were interpreted by Norman lawyers, and adapted over the ages to changing circumstances with much subtlety and ingenuity, this is perhaps the closest we can come to a purely secular version of natural law. Here is no appeal to the eternal or the supernatural, but an appeal rather to the accumulated experience of men who were trying to use their reason as purely as possible. Laws based on such experience stand a good chance of being accepted by those who are subject to them—with the proviso that even such laws can grow so stuffy, bending to changing conditions so slowly, that they too can breed a revolutionary discontent. Since nothing lasts, and all worldly institutions are makeshift, there is no final protection from revolution.

We suggest that in a free society law may be accepted as the rule of reason, or of such reason as the community can scrape together. If it is not accepted it is not law, for it will not be obeyed. Only in a tyrant state can the unacceptable become law, enforced by the secret police at midnight.

'Law in the lawyers' sense,' wrote Oliver Wendell Holmes, 'is a statement of the circumstances in which the public force will be brought to bear upon a man through the Courts.' But the public force will only be brought to bear, in a democracy, when the public believes that the law is reasonable. The public may be inflamed with prejudice and the law may seem to others to be most unreasonable—as with the segregation laws in Alabama today. Strictly speaking these are non-laws, having been declared unconstitutional. But they can still be half-enforced because the local majority still dreams that they are in accord with the facts.

Reason, as a sanction, leaves the subject open for discussion and thus for change. If the sanction is force (Holmes's army or Hobbes's absolutism), there is nothing to discuss except whether the force is adequate to repress dissent. Hobbes makes this clear. He dismisses the plain man's reason (as a source of evil rather than of good), and claims that the only protection for humanity is the absolute state with unlimited powers from which there can be no appeal. Furthermore, the state must organise public opinion to suit itself. Whatever is useful for the State is good; whatever hinders the State is bad. Most men and women are merely things to be used for the benefit of the state. 'The passengers exist for the sake of the ship.'

Hobbes's tyranny could be described as 'the rule of law', as a state in which the laws are clearly defined, and are not overridden by the executive, and are applied to all men impartially by incorruptible courts. Yet there is no freedom. So if the rule of law is to be treated as one of man's essential freedoms (as John Strachey treats it), we must add that the sanction of these laws should be reason—or what will be accepted by the 'reasonable man' as understood in the Common Law. Holmes's 'public force' may then be brought to bear through the courts, with the minimum of harm.

The great Edward Coke, early in the seventeenth century, wrote that the English Common Law is 'nothing else but reason'. This is perhaps too hopeful; but in any case that law is bravely based on a belief in man's reasonable nature—a belief that has much virtue, for if we assume the common reasonableness of man we assume a standard which transcends the differences of race, religion and tradition. So we at least have something to work with in trying to understand other nations and to make ourselves understood. We even have an answer to the trick question which is so often flung at those who believe that force is not the essence of law: 'Is it, then, the duty of the individual to pass judgment on laws before he obeys them?' The answer, in a free society, is 'yes and no'. 'Yes' in trivial matters, such as many regulations dealing with motor cars where there is no point in making a fuss, or in ridiculous matters such as American Prohibition where the law was passed by cheating and was not even supposed to represent the will of the people; but 'no' in matters of substance, since the free man can agitate and seek to persuade his neighbours that the law in question is not just.

Only in an open society, where argument is not suppressed and where reason is alleged to rule, can men willingly obey laws which they believe to be mistaken; for they have every chance to protest and to be heard without risking the annoyance of going to jail. (But when reason is suspended, as it was in the British male's attitude toward votes for women, obedience is suspended also.)

This distinction between the rule of law backed by reason —or by what Jefferson called 'the common sense of things'— and the rule of law backed by force, is vital because the rule of law is not only an essential freedom, it is also the essence of justice.

Any modern man, living under free institutions, if asked to define justice, would probably say something like the following: Justice not only demands equal treatment of all citizens before the law; it also demands that the law does not favour individual citizens or classes, that the courts should be impartial, and that the legal limitations upon freedom should be the minimum which are needed for the protection of society. Emmanuel Kant put the last point succinctly. 'A just constitution,' he wrote, 'is a constitution which achieves the greatest possible freedom of human individuals by framing the laws in such a way that the freedom of each can coexist with that of all others.'

This may sound trite; but in man's long political history it is well-nigh revolutionary, since it defines justice wholly in terms of the individual citizen and not at all in terms of the state. Plato would have been horrified. In the *Republic* he finds that justice is that conduct, or institution, which preserves the perfect City from the decline and fall which besets all the other works of man. All change must be for the worse, in the perfect City, so whatever promotes changelessness promotes justice. And since Plato's perfect City is divided rigidly into three classes, justice demands the maintenance of this class structure.

We need not argue about what should happen in a perfect City (or state) since we are in no danger of seeing one. But we should notice that even for Plato, the great idealist, the passengers exist for the sake of the ship. The City must be preserved untouched, although most of the citizens are thus condemned forever to servile labour. This would be the fascist view, and it appears to be the view of all Communist states. And, although it is deadly to freedom and to democracy alike, it has been the prevailing view throughout most of human history. It has been so long 'in the air' that we must daily guard lest it contaminate our own thoughts. Most people can read Plato's *Republic*, with its persuasive style and its many beautiful sentiments, without noticing that they are reading a totalitarian tract.

4

The other two freedoms proclaimed, or foretold, by Franklin Roosevelt are freedom from want and freedom from fear. Perhaps in 1941 the President really felt some hope for such freedoms. In the midst of fearful wars men tend to think that after victory the world will be a better place, in spite of the obvious fact that it must become a worse place. A great war settles (but at a price) exactly what it is intended to settle: which of two power-groups shall have charge of the immediate future. The hopes of man may depend on the 'right' group winning, in which case the war must be fought; but we have no excuse for assuming that the world will be a better place when so many good men are dead and so many noble cities are rubble. Still, Roosevelt must have made that assumption when he talked about 'freedom from want, through economic understanding—*everywhere in the world*. Freedom from fear, through world-wide reduction of armaments—*everywhere in the world.*' The statement of such an ambition sounds sarcastic today.

First, half our world is in want and there is little economic understanding, even among good friends. Instead, we mutely suffer the economic anarchy of nationalism. And the want feeds on itself, since the helplessly destitute have little to do except breed:

> *'The thriftless towns litter with lives undone,*
> *To whom our madness left no joy but one;*
> *And irony that glares like Judgment Day*
> *Sees Men accumulate and Wealth decay.'*

Second, all our world is in fear, and the fear also feeds on itself, preventing the reduction of armaments.

Nevertheless, these presently impossible freedoms may become a major problem in the future, if we are to have a future. The first two of Roosevelt's four freedoms (speech and religious worship) deal with each man's right to live and develop in his own fashion. We know how to try to make this form of freedom possible, and in the advanced democracies we come tolerably close to succeeding. But the second two freedoms demand interdependence, demand economic and political organisation on an international scale. The first are the individual freedoms and the second the collective. To some extent the second freedoms (freedom from fear and want) may even limit the first, since they require a form of social organisation, at home and with friendly neighbours, which means both a diminution of personal independence and a limitation of national sovereignty.

If we are to seek such Utopian pleasures as freedom from want and from fear we shall have to subject ourselves to the discipline of living amicably with all sorts of strange foreigners and of sacrificing some of our national selfishness and personal egotism.

'Can our conception of civilisation,' asked Roussy de Sales, 'which rests finally on the principle of individual freedom, be reconciled with our knowledge that both war and want can be eliminated only through collective discipline?' There may be no escape from this dilemma of freedom versus efficiency (or of one's personal freedom to do as one chooses versus the world's freedom from want). As in so much of political life, we may have to veer forever between one unsatisfactory alternative and the other. No one has promised us a happy ending. But this does not mean that freedom ceases to be the absolute toward which we strive. It means that the collective freedoms are sometimes so important to the survival of humanity that they justify a curtailment of the individual ones—but only a curtailment. The collective must never suppress the individual freedoms, for the latter embody all our frail hopes for human progress.

2
Representative Democracy

WE HAVE SEEN the dangers of the many freedoms which we have enjoyed and have sought to protect. These dangers, these anti-freedoms, will beset any society which seeks the blessings of liberty and the blessings of good government and security side by side. The new nations will have to grapple with the anti-freedoms one by one. They will be wise if they study our long story of semi-failure and semi-success; for no other, no undiscovered, form of freedom exists— except the freedom of the savage which in despite of Rousseau is probably the most brief and painful form of human life. Nevertheless, if the perils of freedom are manifold, the perils of democracy (our best defender of freedom) can easily match them.

We found it impossible to discuss freedom, which is based upon law, without asking what is the nature of law and what is the sanction we are prepared to accept. Similarly, we cannot discuss democracy, which is embodied in many of our nation-states, without reference to the form of nationalism which has conquered most of the world since the French Revolution. We shall try to suggest that this is more a curse than a blessing; but we cannot deny that it is the major fact in modern political history. It is also very new in its present form. This allows us to hope that it may be transcended before it frustrates our civilisation.

Today, however, all our democracies are nation-states. This seems the only political form which can gather the affection and devotion that are needed to hold a community together. Yet the nation-state is the enemy to peace, the enemy to large-scale systems of order, and thus the negation of democracy which must conquer the anarchy of the nations or be conquered by it. Patriotism is health-giving and does not exclude a loyalty to the human race. Nationalism is organised selfishness and in its shadow humanitarian feelings gradually dissolve. 'My country right or wrong' is not a democratic slogan.

2

In tribal communities, and even in the advanced societies of Greece and of the Roman Republic, defeat in war often meant total ruin, as with Carthage, or a combination of death and slavery, as with the island of Melos. Neutralism or internationalism was impossible. Man's chief duty was to fight for his homeland. If a group neglected this duty it would quickly become the victim of its neighbours.

The Roman Empire made a wider horizon. Men could think of far-off peoples as fellow-citizens. The civilised world was defended, on the distant Wall, by professional troops, while at home there was time for culture, sports and decadence. After the decline of Rome, Europe inherited this notion of a common loyalty—this time to the Church. When the Church split, the carnage was terrible; but still the old dream of unity persisted and by the eighteenth century both tribal and religious wars seemed part of a dark past. Gibbon expressed the prevailing mood as follows, in his *General Observations on the Fall of the Roman Empire in the West*:

'A philosopher may be permitted ... to consider Europe as one great republic, whose various inhabitants have attained almost the same level of politeness and cultivation. The balance of power will continue to fluctuate, and the prosperity of our own, or the neighbouring kingdoms, may be alternately exalted or depressed; but these partial events cannot essentially injure our general state of happiness, the system of arts, and laws, and manners, which so advantageously distinguish, above the rest of mankind, the Europeans and their colonies.... In peace, the progress of knowledge and industry is accelerated by the emulation of so many active rivals: in war, the European forces are exercised by temperate and undecisive contests.'

Life, as usual, was playing the Chestertonian game of 'cheat the prophet'. The last volume of *The Decline and Fall* was published in 1788. The following year the Bastille was stormed, and within thirteen years Hegel was teaching at the University of Jena. In the name of liberty the French resurrected the fanatical state-worship of Sparta and married it to the wild forces of revolution. In the name of divine monarchy Hegel deified the mythical racial-state and bound the citizens in iron chains to its service. The kings and the liberty-caps have departed; but the new nationalism remains to threaten our freedoms, and perhaps to incubate the final war.

The French law of mobilisation in 1793 proclaims: 'Henceforth, until the enemies have been driven from the soil of France, all Frenchmen are permanently on call for the service of the armies. The young will go to battle; married men will make arms and move supplies; women will make tents and clothes and will serve in the hospitals; children will turn rags into lint; old men will be carried into the public squares to raise the courage of the warriors, to preach hatred of kings and the unity of the Republic.'

Arnold Toynbee comments: 'Thus, at one stroke of baleful magic, the French state is transformed from a public utility into a goddess.' Over-excited by that strange goddess, Marie Joseph Chénier told the Convention: 'On the ruins of the dethroned superstitions can be founded the one natural religion, having neither sects nor mysteries. Her preachers are our legislators, her priests our executive officers of the state. In the temple of this religion humanity will offer incense only on the altar of our country, the mother of us all and our divinity.'

A harsh mother and an Old Testament divinity, for those who disagree are not cajoled, are not disciplined, they are killed. 'One dare not hope,' said Saint-Just to the Convention, 'that things will improve so long as one foe of freedom breathes.... After the French people had announced its will everything which is contrary to its will stands outside the sovereignty of the nation; and who stands outside the sovereign in his enemy.' But who on earth are these 'people'? Anyone who has ever looked about him knows that people are endlessly variable, unequal in their talents, divided in their interests, their amusements and their wants, and generally as unlike each other as can be. They are not Norway lemmings; they are troublesome individuals who have no common will to announce. What Saint-Just meant was that *he* knew exactly what the people wanted. In the name of that confidence he and his friends held power briefly until Napoleon took over. But the myth of the mother-nation, the divinity, lingered on.

An intelligent and truthful Communist, who clearly thought himself humane, was challenged to explain some elections in his home-country, Rumania. 'Surely', he was asked, 'that well-nigh unanimous vote showed that the elections were rigged?' 'Of course they were rigged', he answered, sounding baffled and almost shocked. 'It was right that they should be. It was our duty to the people, who are still too ignorant to be trusted to vote Communist.' Here, as in the case of Saint-Just, the State knew what was right—the State being personified by a few men who had established power over the many and who may well have believed that by maintaining that power they were doing good.

'Children belong to the Republic', announced Barère at the height of the Revolution. 'The Republic leaves to parents the guidance of your first years, but as soon as your intelligence forms itself the Republic proudly claims the rights it holds over you. You are born for the Republic.' Hitler took much the same view. 'The era of personal happiness is closed', he said, meaning that thenceforward the life of the citizen must be wholly devoted to the power and glory of the State.

Carlton Hayes, in *The Historical Evolution of Modern Nationalism*, sums up: ' "The People" has become "the nation", a mystical entity, an absolute sovereign, a Moloch not only of classes but of individuals. It catechises its own citizens, and by force it seeks to catechise the citizens of other nations.... It can seize everything and destroy everything, for above it there is no law.... It has a horror of divisions, schisms, minorities. It labours for unity, uniformity, concentration.... Its vaunted liberty, in the last analysis, is not for the individual but for the National State. The nation may do whatever it will; the individual may do only what the National State determines.'

There is little room for our Western freedoms in such a society; but even the Revolution is kindly when compared to the State which Hegel advocated. The Revolution suppressed freedom in the name of liberty, equality, and the brotherhood of man. The good ideas might one day triumph over the bad practice. But Hegel sought to suppress freedom in the name of the Prussian reaction which followed the exit of Napoleon. He too taught that the State is everything, the individual nothing. 'The State is the Divine Idea as it exists on earth', wrote Hegel. And again: 'We must worship the State as the manifestation of the Divine on earth.... The State is the march of God through the world.' It exists for its own sake, he adds, and only in the State (or through the State) can we realise our moral life.

These notions must have pleased King Frederick William III of Prussia, who by 1818 had called Hegel to the professorship of philosophy at Berlin. Hegel had tamed the wild nationalism of the Revolution and turned it into a disciplined worship of the Prussian State. No wonder the modern totalitarians have been grateful to Hegel. He remade the revolt against freedom into a movement of the austere Spartan type; the totalitarians remade it again into a popular frenzy; but it was the same old revolt.

The State, for Hegel, is the moral law, as well as all the other types of law. Here is Hitler, and all the snivelling in the dock at Nuremberg about 'obeying orders'. Here too is Stalin. Here would be Mussolini, had he succeeded in building a genuine State. And here is the death of freedom. For such a State cannot be judged by any outside standard, least of all by that of individual or 'bourgeois' morality. The only test is success, which is to be measured by the power of the State—and by the terror which it spreads abroad lest the power be challenged. As for other States, which might have ideas of their own: 'When the particular wills of the States can come to no agreement,' wrote Hegel, 'their controversy can be decided only by war.' And in war, presumably, the Hegelian or Spartan State should always win, since the entire life of the community has been devoted to the service of what should be, in Toynbee's phrase, a public utility.

A trivial example may help to illustrate the shame of this view of life. When freedom is to be suppressed (or ignored, in a community which professes freedom) the historian is one of the first to be muzzled. Among the crimes of nationalism not the least are the text-books from which the 'histories' of the nation-states are taught. In many American communities the legislators have one firm conviction; namely, that the United States have never been wrong, have never been cruel, have never been unfair and have never been beaten at anything. And the same legislators often have the power to forbid the use of a book in the local educational system. The results are not as bad as they might be, since the legislators are negligent and many of them prefer not to read books. But what would happen if the sources of knowledge were controlled by well-educated and diligent servants of an Hegelian State, servants who believed whole-heartedly that the State could do no wrong and that its leaders were therefore semi-sacred? We have a partial answer in Russia.*

When it seemed that Malenkov was to succeed the dead Stalin, *Pravda* published a photograph showing him with Stalin and Mao Tse-tung. The same picture had been published three years earlier, but with Malenkov in a far humbler position, not at the dictator's elbow. When Beria was shot as a spy, the *Large Soviet Encyclopaedia* sent all its subscribers an article on the Bering Straits. This was to replace the entry on the 'traitor' Beria. The 1938 edition of the *Short Course*

* The following facts are taken from *The Times* of London.

on Soviet history naturally glorified Stalin and treated his critics as either non-existent or Satanic. This was the 'truth' until Khrushchev began his de-Stalinisation campaign. Then, in the revised *Short Course*, the once all-powerful hero was moved into an inconspicuous background. And today the *History of the Communist Party of the Soviet Union* is being withdrawn from circulation so that Khrushchev himself may become a minor figure whose kindly masters occasionally allowed him to make speeches but who never amounted to anything.

All this may seem a joke; but if the Russians do such things to each other, imagine what they do to us. And imagine the difficulty a well-meaning Russian citizen must have in seeing the outside world as anything but a conglomeration of demons who are all plotting against the USSR, subverting farmers to produce inadequate crops and in general poisoning the wells of life. As soon as a society admits, or is kicked into admitting, that the first and last aim of politics is the power of the State, not only do justice and freedom disappear, but also man's inadequate but sincere efforts towards impartial history. And a people without a reasonably honest history are like a man without a memory but with an abundance of mad fantasies.

So both the ferment of the French Revolution, and the reaction which followed, promoted the new nation-state. Except for the convenience of tyrants a self-centred State is an anomaly in a world of vast economic units and of weapons which threaten every living object. It is an extra-anomaly in our Western world which seeks freedom (which can never mean simply *my* freedom, since no man not a savage can be free all by himself) and which professes democracy (which is the creed of brotherhood).

To serve democracy we need a combined loyalty: to our country and to the human race (or to as much of the human race as is willing to converse with us). In their own way the Communists have sought this larger loyalty. But they will only converse with people who agree on Communism, whereas we must seek and encourage *dis*agreement if we are to keep our minds and our politics vigorous.

One last complaint against egotistical nationalism: it makes for dangerous rigidity in foreign relations. Once a 'right' or a 'principle' has been proclaimed in the name of the State (or still worse, 'a matter of national interest'), the most tranquil democracy becomes inflamed and cantankerous. Hence the prevalence of wars. Bonar Law said, 'There is no such thing as inevitable war. If war comes it will be from the failure of human wisdom.' He should have added 'or the failure of human institutions', for the self-satisfied, self-glorifying National State *breeds* wars. Hegel, as we have seen, declared that when the wills of two States disagree 'their controversy can be decided only by war'. This is because States, even would-be democratic States, talk about absolute rights and wrongs which cannot be compromised or even discussed quietly. The extreme claim, once made, cannot be relinquished. The rulers cannot resort to Gibbon's 'temperate and undecisive contests'. Like duellists, rather than statesmen, they are compelled to press for victory or defeat. Examples of such contests are the American wars against Mexico and Spain, the Crimean and the Boer wars, possibly even the vast Civil War in the United States. (We omit the Franco-Prussian War because a pure Hegelian State was involved, and for such a State war is not a tragedy but a good thing.)

If all national states are touchy and inflexible in foreign affairs, democratic national states are feckless as well. No matter how wise the rulers, no modern democracy can keep its armed forces together after victory. Both Britain and America, in 1945, succumbed to the immature notion that power could be put into cold storage now that the war was 'won'. The years of sacrifice and bereavement might have been a game which was now ended. The score was posted; the victors were acknowledged; so why not go home? Neither Prime Minister nor President, nor all the generals together, could have kept the troops from laying down their arms nor the voters at home from insisting upon this folly. The Russian people, on the other hand, were not consulted; they were given orders which they obeyed.

And if democracies go home too soon, they also tend to go to war too late. No leaders can budge them, in a neck-or-nothing crisis, until they feel that their own farms, their own industries, their own habits of life are threatened. Thus they will usually start their wars unprepared. This is the price of freedom and it cannot be dodged.

3

One by one the new nations are falling into the trap of nationalism. They equate 'freedom' with the absence of colonial rule and do not think to demand their own basic freedoms from their own State. They copy what is bad in the West and ignore what is good: they copy nationalism and ignore civil liberties. A new flag at the United Nations means more to them than the right to think and talk and worship and assemble as they choose, and to protest with all vigour short of mayhem. They may therefore find that their new subjection, to their own chosen masters, is more burdensome than their old.

As we watch the tragedy we should not comment smugly that such simple people are only fit for strong and ruthless government. We should remind ourselves that their plight is partly our own fault. We taught them the wrong religion: not freedom, which we serve at best with half our hearts, but nationalism and the worship of the sovereign State.

Could we but clear our minds of French Revolutionary and Hegelian jargon, and look about us candidly, we would see that we have no need for this concept of the State, or for the nationalism which is its shadow. Today an attack on nationalism is construed as an attack on patriotism or on one's own country. In fact it is an attack on an abstraction which hinders freedom and promotes slavery.

All we need, for a democratic picture of the political world, are two concepts. First, the concept of a country (or a nation): the community in which one was born. The citizens of this community may be easier to understand, and to cherish, than foreigners. The sights and sounds and habits, the food and the drink and the prejudices, may be close to one's heart. The institutions may please or infuriate, but in any case they are one's own institutions which one must guard or change (or both) for one's own sake and for the sake of one's children. This is the concept of home. And the second is the concept of limited government, meaning government which accepts restraint upon its use of power for the sake of the individual, the humble citizen, who must not be coerced or twisted except for the protection of other citizens.

There is no room here for the State as understood by Barère and Hegel, or by Stalin and Hitler. The fact is that for a democracy which is seeking to promote freedom the State does not exist. Patriotism supplants nationalism. Government supplants the 'Divine Idea' of the State. No barrier remains to prevent us from co-operating with our friendly neighbours—on the lines which Roosevelt must have imagined when he dreamed of freedom from fear and want. No barrier, that is, except our old bad habits, our selfishness, our avarice, our ignorance, our parochial distaste for foreigners and for 'abroad'. These we may hope to outgrow some day. At least no one prevents us from trying.

If we can stick to the two workaday concepts of home and government, forgetting God and Destiny for the moment, there is nothing to keep us from wooing our hostile neighbours also, reminding them that we do not picture our country as 'the march of God through the world', but merely as a pleasant place to live and work and bring up children, and to improve wherever we are able, a place which we shall defend at any cost but from which we shall launch no intended evil.

Unintended evil, however, we launch all day long, chiefly upon the bewildered heads of the ex-colonial peoples. We are learning, through harsh experience, that the National State is obsolete and that it threatens to erase man's future. Simultaneously, we encourage the newly-freed peoples to bind themselves into the very trap from which we seek escape. We have as yet no other model to offer them. Belatedly, we are trying to find a new basis for political life and for the relations between large political units. Meanwhile we welcome the new nations into the old system which is half-collapsed. In the name of national self-interest they too will soon be destroying their children's hopes. Perhaps it is a pity that they were liberated before the tardy democracies admitted that science has made their jealous little States ridiculous.

4

The concept of a home-country is clear enough; but what of the concept of a government divorced from 'worship of the Divine on earth' and thus from absolute power? The modern substitute for the Greek system wherein all citizens were legislators (and on occasion judges-and-juries also) is representative government—a paraphrase, today, for constitutional democracy. In other words, when we speak of democracy and liberty we mean the imperfect embodiment of those ideals in the representative governments we see about us. Walter Lippmann warns us not to take the name for the reality. 'Merely to enfranchise the voters,' he writes, 'even to give them a true representation, will not in itself establish self-government; it may just as well lead, and in most countries has in fact led, to a new form of absolute State, a self-perpetuating oligarchy and an uncontrollable bureaucracy which governs by courting, cajoling, corrupting and coercing the sovereign but incompetent people.'

And elsewhere he writes, 'We must assume as a theoretically fixed premise of popular government that normally men as members of a public will not be well informed, continuously interested, non-partisan, creative or executive'. This is a more modest pessimism than that of David Hume, who said that 'political writers have established it as a maxim, that, in contriving any system of government, and fixing the several checks and controls of the constitution, *every man* ought to be supposed a knave'. Even Jefferson, the hero of democracy, agreed. 'Free government,' he said, 'is founded in jealousy and not in confidence.'

Before asking how far our systems and constitutions protect us from erring human nature we must try to see exactly what representative government means. The idea is simple: the people, who are too numerous and far-scattered to be present at the seat of government in person, are present by proxy through their elected officers. This is all very well for that useful abstraction, 'the people'. But what of the individual 'person' whose chosen candidate is never elected and who is never represented by a man with whom he agrees? That is part of the game; he is assumed to be represented and the assumption is a small price to pay for an orderly constitutional system. In the words of Winston Churchill, we must be thankful for the 'enormous and unquestionably helpful part that humbug plays in the social life of great peoples dwelling in a state of democratic freedom'.

Historically, the decisive step toward free government comes when the representatives of the people get control of public spending. Thenceforth the executive (King, President or Prime Minister), be he ever so wilful, can only do those things for which money has been provided. In theory, if the executive becomes too haughty or unpopular, he can be starved of funds. *The Federalist* puts the theory with precision: 'This power over the purse may, in fact, be regarded as the most complete and effectual weapon with which any constitution can arm the immediate representatives of the people, for obtaining a redress of every grievance, and for carrying into effect every just and salutary measure.'

Here, too, a good deal of 'humbug' has arisen over the years. In Britain the Members of Parliament of the majority party must swallow whatever budget is handed to them. They may object to being rubber stamps; but they continue in their humble duty of stamping. In the United States, where party discipline does not prevail in Congress and where the Chief Executive is elected for a fixed term, the Congress may treat a budget roughly and hash it about to such an extent that the hopes and plans of the President are thwarted; but no alternative plans are put in their place. This occasional scuffle can scarcely be described as the redress of grievances, still less as 'carrying into effect every just and salutary measure'. Yet in both countries the 'power over the purse' is still indirectly in the hands of the representatives —because of the Opposition.

In Great Britain an unpopular government will soon fall and be replaced by the Opposition. In the United States the same will happen at the next Presidential election—which may be years, or only months, away. Then comes the time for 'the redress of grievances', and even (if the nation is very lucky) for 'salutary measures'. Thus representative government as practised in the English-speaking world cannot exist without an Opposition, without an organised group which can take over and carry on the public business. How else could we express our discontent and 'get the rascals out'? Yet this dependence on an Opposition is not a necessity for free political life, as the Swiss have shown us; so we should not be too contemptuous of the Asian or African nations who do not understand our sophisticated device. They may find some other way to control the insolence of power.

For us, however, the right to choose a government is inseparable from the right to dismiss it—and this we cannot do unless we have the right to organise more than one political party. This seemingly innocuous 'right' is denied to half the human race. The Communists justify this denial on the grounds that political parties represent class interests and that a Communist State, which knows only one class, needs only one party. If this were true it would mean that no one in a Communist country would feel the impulse to organise a second party. Yet the laws against this non-existent impulse are strict and the penalties for doing what nobody would want to do are extreme. On the whole we may assume that the absence of an alternative party, in any society, means the presence of tyranny. (The Swiss, although they do not have our form of Opposition, do have a variety of parties.)*

The British speak of 'the Leader of Her Majesty's Loyal Opposition', a phrase which Communists find ridiculous and which many leaders of the new nations call hypocritical. For them, opposition means total opposition, which in turn means revolution. They cannot grasp that a man may be fiercely loyal to the British system of government (and thus to the Queen) and at the same time fiercely opposed to what the temporary leaders of that government are doing. We should not wonder that this puzzles the Africans and annoys the Communists. The idea is complicated. It is also new, as we can see by looking at the formative years of the government of the United States.

Perplexed and alienated by the acerbity of British politics, the makers of the American Constitution trusted that their new country could do without the political parties which they equated with mere cliques and factions. Washington, in his *Farewell Address*, lent his mighty name to this view. 'I have already intimated to you', he said, 'the danger of parties in the State.... Let me now take a more comprehensive view, and warn you in the most solemn manner against the baneful effects of the spirit of party generally.... It serves always to distract the public councils and enfeeble the public administration. It agitates the community with ill-founded jealousies and false alarms; kindles the animosity of one part against another; foments occasional riot and insurrection.' The last phrase is interesting, since the Americans were to have trouble, at first, in distinguishing between party spirit and treason.

Needless to say, parties developed at once in America. There is no freedom in electing a government unless you can

* See pp. 84–5.

throw it out and put another in its place. Along with the parties came the party press. Political conflict was soon as rancorous in the ex-colonies as in the mother-country. In 1798 a Sedition Act was passed, under which a number of Opposition editors were fined or imprisoned for bringing members of the Government 'into contempt or disrepute'—which it was their business to do. The foolish law, which led to turmoil and soon fell into disuse, was a sign that the party in power did not yet see that the Opposition may be loyal to the country while striving continually to bring the Administration into 'disrepute'.

John Strachey once wrote, 'I was told that the only translation into many African languages of the phrase "the leader of the Opposition" was "*chief enemy*"!' The Americans quickly recovered from this aberration and ceased putting opposition spokesmen into jail.

5

The problem of freedom is institutional: we must tame the power of government without diminishing it. The executive must have all powers needed to safeguard and to promote the well-being of the people, yet the powers must not be used except by permission. Thus our key-institution is representative government, the only system we know which can serve this double purpose.

No matter how the Parliament or Congress or Assembly is elected, it will not be representative in fact unless it is seen as a system of trusteeship, which means clear responsibility and strict accounting. Such a system presupposes at least two conditions. First, the voters in every party should be as free as possible to choose whom they will to represent them. To whatever extent the choice is limited, the voter must settle for what he can get rather than for what he would like. The voters in England, for instance, have a far wider choice than those in the United States where the representative is expected to be a resident of his state or district. And second, the supervision by the representative body, by the trustees, must extend over the whole field of government. This means that if permissive powers are given to the executive (powers not immediately subject to control by the Assembly), they should be given only in emergency and only for the shortest possible time.

Ideally there should be a third condition: that the representative body, as in Britain, should meet the administration face to face. This was intended, in a modified form, by the founders of the American Republic. Their Constitution left the heads of executive departments free to go before the Congress and defend their proposed measures. When the Congress, after a brief experiment, refused to receive these officers, the separation of powers became inordinate. Yet the American Government clearly works, so the third condition is clearly not essential.*

Before discussing the inherent dangers of representative government, we must justify our assumption that freedom depends upon political institutions. Marx would disagree. (Incidentally, wherever we refer to Marx we mean the man himself as seen in his works: a great humanitarian, a fallible economist and an historian who went astray by confusing history with prophecy. This remarkable man should not be held responsible for the practices of the Communist States which we face today.)

The quarrel of the free world with Karl Marx has nothing to do with Russians or Chinese or other betrayers of Marxism; it has to do with the theory of history and of power. Marx believed that he had founded a science of history and economics which made it possible to foresee the future. A future which can be predicted must be inevitable. If events and circumstances cannot be altered, there is not

* The Constitution of the Confederate States, adopted at the outbreak of the Civil War after seventy years of experience with the older document, authorised a law to permit the heads of executive departments to sit in Congress and take part in the discussion of measures affecting their work.

much point in politics. Marx admitted that we might 'shorten the birthpangs' of the inevitable by political action; but do what we may the baby must be born and its shape and colour must be such as Marx foretold.

The future was to be discerned in economic class-relationships and in the evolution of the material means of production. So the horrors of the early days of an industrial revolution—which Marx had deplored in England and which were later to be far exceeded during the Communist industrialisation of Russia and of China—could not be assuaged by politics. They must be conquered by the 'inevitable' next stage in history which would produce the classless society.

For those who serve freedom here and now, rather than in the formless future, this is the ultimate heresy. We believe that political power, so far from being helpless before economic power and before pieces of machinery, is the key to all power and the only device for promoting justice and liberty.

Marx dismissed the democracy of his day as 'mere formal freedom'. He was scarcely exaggerating. *Das Kapital* (the first volume) was published at Hamburg in 1867. This was the year of the Second Reform Bill which gave the vote to British householders who lived in their houses and paid the rates—adding about 1,353,000 voters to the electorate. Lord Cranbourne (later the great Lord Salisbury) called the bill 'a very dangerous experiment'. He and two colleagues resigned from the Cabinet in protest. Meanwhile in the United States, which were on the verge of the unbuttoned licentiousness of the robber-baron days, the Congress was seeking to impeach President Andrew Johnson because of his efforts to treat the defeated Southerners like human beings. The attack on Johnson has been described by two eminent historians as 'one of the most disgraceful and vulgar episodes in the history of the Federal Government'. Democracy was not behaving at its best while Marx sat in the British Museum writing his book.

Marx claimed to read the future, yet he did not foresee

the most important event in the long, tumultuous history of government. In his day representative government existed not only in theory but in practice. In his day the franchise was being extended in England and had been extended in America. During his prophetic moods, if he had only chosen to imagine that one day all men and women would have the vote and that one day representative government would be developed to the point where it could do its task with moderate efficiency—what a democrat he might have been!*
And how much he could have taught us about making our cranky system work. All he wanted was to free men so far as possible from 'the kingdom of necessity' so that they might spend an ever larger part of their lives in 'the kingdom of freedom' which 'begins only where drudgery, enforced by hardship and by external purposes, ends'.

Perhaps Marx had suffered so much from the experience of his time that he could no longer hope for economic improvement except by cataclysmic change. Perhaps he was impatient and could not wait on the slowly-spreading institutions of freedom but felt he must prove at once to the oppressed that a rosy future was inevitable. Perhaps he was consoling himself, escaping from the responsibility of political action into a future dream-paradise which was 'scientifically' certain. In any case we lost him, and the loss is grievous.

The 'mere formal freedom' which Marx brushed aside as just another feeble excuse for the *status quo* has developed into our only known contrivance for preventing the misuse of power and for controlling the class-tensions and the ever-changing material means of production which Marx thought would overwhelm, and in the end abolish, politics. But now that we have found and developed this contrivance we have the task of supervising it, of seeing that it is used to protect freedom. In bad hands it could enslave us overnight. Professor Sir Karl Popper writes:

* He did live to write ' . . . all I know is that I am not a Marxist'. *Selected Correspondence of Marx and Engels* 1846–95. London, 1934.

'We must think in these matters in even more materialist terms, as it were, than Marx did. We must realise that the control of physical power and of physical exploitation remains the central political problem. In order to establish this control, we must establish "merely formal freedom". Once we have achieved this, and have learned how to use it for the control of political power, everything rests with us. We must not blame anybody else any longer, nor cry out against the sinister economic demons behind the scenes. For in a democracy we hold the keys to the control of the demons. We can tame them. We must realise this and use the keys: we must construct institutions for the democratic control of economic power, and for our protection from economic exploitation.'

This is all true. But is it also impossible, as Marx would have insisted? Here we come hard against the greatest weakness of democracy, which is indifference, or human laziness. Freedom is troublesome and tyranny is the easy way out.

The suffrage itself has defects which can never be remedied since they are part of human nature. We do not cast our votes with detached wisdom. We vote because of personal interest, class interest, the influence of friends or superiors, and prejudices which may be ineradicable because they are unconscious. How can we assume that, after millions of such votes, the bad and selfish elements will cancel each other and only a good element, which we call 'the voice of the people', will remain? Similarly, our representative institutions might mirror every weakness and corruption of which man is capable; but they are more likely to mirror a gross mediocrity. Yet we expect them to rise well above the average of human attainment, in spite of the fact that we seldom live up to our own responsibilities. What guardian angel watches over democracy? And for how long?

So far, it is unquestionably Marx who missed the boat, not us. If we compare our world, in terms of freedom and democracy, with the world which Marx dismissed contemptuously in 1867, the contrast startles. Marx's capitalism is dead, along with *laissez faire*. We have somehow built a mixed and managed economy, under effective political control, which works more often than it fails and which allows more people to spend more of their lives in the 'kingdom of freedom' than was ever dreamed in the past. Our piecemeal and unpredicted tinkering with the society of which Marx despaired has made us an object of envy to many of the so-called 'Marxian' countries. They are more likely, today, to copy our pragmatic experiments than we are to copy their revealed religion.

We might even indulge in cautious optimism were it not for nationalism, the bomb, and doubts as to whether we are capable for long of bearing the load of freedom.

First, nationalism. Our best hope is that some day we may return to the sobriety of 1945 when we still felt an obligation toward those who had died during six years of war. In 1945 Dr T. V. Soong (who unfortunately spoke for a moribund regime) offered to yield any necessary part of China's sovereignty so that the United Nations might have power unmarred by vetoes. And Anthony Eden said in the House of Commons, 'Every succeeding scientific discovery makes greater nonsense of old-time conceptions of sovereignty.' And Michael Foot wrote for a New York newspaper, 'What is required is a deliberate resignation of sovereignty.' And Robert Oppenheimer wrote, "It is a practical thing to recognise as a common responsibility, wholly incapable of unilateral solution, the completely common peril that atomic weapons constitute for the world, to recognise that only by a community of responsibility is there any hope of meeting that peril.' And Harold Stassen, perennial candidate for the Presidency of the United States, told the Academy of Political Science, 'The world needed government on a world level before the atomic bomb. Now it has become an imperative.' And the *Saturday Review* announced in New York: 'He (Man) shall have to recognise the flat truth that the greatest obsolescence of all in the Atomic Age is national sovereignty.' Where are those words today? 'Far too far off for thought or any prayer.' In twenty years we have closed our minds to what we once saw clearly, that the choice is between nationalism and death.

Second, the bomb. If we choose to be hopeful we may repeat the words of Winston Churchill: 'It may well be that we shall by a process of sublime irony have reached a stage in this story where safety will be the sturdy child of terror and survival the twin brother of annihilation.'

Third, have we the strength to carry the burden of our democracy? That we cannot foretell. The burden is not light: 'We must not blame anybody else any longer, nor cry out against the sinister economic demons behind the scenes. For in a democracy we hold the keys.'

While learning to use those keys we should not flatter ourselves that we can serve freedom by making people more kind or more unselfish. Various religions have tried this without noticeably increasing the proportion of the highminded. We have no time to cure the human race; but good political institutions can make society more wholesome in a single generation—leaving men as they are, but protecting their weakness and encouraging their respect for justice. *The New Yorker* put the point neatly: 'Do not try to save the world by loving thy neighbour; it will only make him nervous. Save the world by respecting thy neighbour's rights under law and insisting that he respect yours (under the same law).'

Thus the burden is thrown back upon us. The aimless search for 'better men in politics' or 'a higher political morality' can go on indefinitely. It requires no effort beyond lip-service, which is restful. But the search for a clearer definition and a deeper understanding of the politics of freedom is laborious and urgent. If we give nothing but lip-service here, we can quickly lose all we have gained over centuries of experiment. Slowly, and with many lapses, we have come a long way; but we can slump back in a few indolent years to where we started.

'The fact of progress is written plain and large on the page of history,' wrote H. A. L. Fisher when contemplating his own *History of Europe*, 'but progress is not a law of nature. The ground gained by one generation may be lost by the next. The thoughts of men may flow into the channels which lead to disaster and barbarism.'

We have watched this happen in the case of the Nazis. The worst members of that gang reverted, in less than a generation, to where *homo sapiens* began. Yet we need not be discouraged by this astonishing performance. The same German stock which was debauched by the institutions of National Socialism has produced many of America's best citizens when living under an imperfect version of constitutional, representative government. There is no law of progress, and no promise of it, but the law of decline and fall should be clear to every reader of history. It can only be evaded, from year to year, by careful and step-by-step planning of ever better institutions to safeguard our democracy. We cannot stand still. And the first slip may mean a return to darkness.

6

Throughout this book we have asserted the need for a clearer definition of our Western form of democracy. How close can we come to meeting this need?

We must begin with a negative: democracy is not simply 'the rule of the people' or 'the rule of the majority'. The majority can be as oppressive as a tyrant, and can thus be anti-democratic. To simplify, we may say that only two forms of government are possible: democracy on the one hand, and on the other hand some form of arbitrary and despotic power. Thus an oppressive, impatient and overbearing majority is in fact a tyrannous mob.

Democracy, in our sophisticated Western sense, can never be mere head-counting. It is a set of institutions which establish public control of the Executive through the

Assembly's power over the purse, and which permit the people to get rid of the whole lot (Executive and Assembly alike) without bloodshed. The last two words are the most important. When the people can obtain radical change without violence, and in the process substitute new rulers for the old without violence, democracy exists. In our Western experience to date, the head-counting elections are a necessary part of this system. But the heart of the matter is found in the institutions which protect today's minorities from oppression and which allow for the peaceful dismissal of yesterday's majority. This means that yesterday's majority, while it was still in power, had the duty to make sure that the Opposition could overthrow it.

Such a system, as the founders of the American Republic reiterated, demands much restraint and virtue from the citizens, and much wisdom and loyalty from the leaders whom the citizens have chosen to follow. Democracy does not deny the existence of natural leaders, does not deny the paramount excellence of a few men at any given time; but it denies that the citizen need applaud or recognise that excellence unless he cares to do so. In 1828, for example, the lucky American voters could choose between two great men for the Presidency: John Quincy Adams and Andrew Jackson. They happily ignored the extraordinary qualities of Adams and elected Jackson with delight. He was their first democratic hero, sprung from the people and with instinctive knowledge of their wants and prejudices. The voters were right in thinking he was their friend. They would have been mad, merely because he was a democrat, to think he was their equal. He ruled his government with a fierce will and a stubborn pride, and the country loved it—but only because Jackson, in spite of his autocratic methods, revered the institutions which had made the country possible.

This interplay is essential to a democracy. The people must welcome the superior man when they can find him; and the superior man must welcome the institutions which control him and which may force him any day into defeat.

If the will of the majority is held to be sovereign and supreme, overriding the written or unwritten Constitution, why should that majority ever accept dismissal? It can easily rig a plebiscite, a meaningless 'yes-or-no' vote, which confirms its illicit power in the name of 'democracy'. The usurper becomes legitimate. The despotism springs from 'the people' who are thenceforth silenced in the name of their own sovereign will. Walter Lippmann calls this confusion between constitutional democracy and the mere will of the majority 'the supreme political heresy of our time'. Yet it is an easy trick to play with language, as Hitler showed us, and plenty of 'bumpkins at the fair' fall for the trick every time.

William Jennings Bryan was such a bumpkin. He displayed his folly, unashamed, at the 'Monkey Trial' in 1925. The legislature of Tennessee had adopted a statute which forbade schools supported by public funds from teaching 'the theory that denies the story of the divine creation of man as taught in the Bible'. When an instructor in biology was prosecuted under this law, Bryan represented the state. He argued that the 'will of the people' must prevail. He secured a conviction, but sentence was set aside amid world-wide mirth—another instance of a law that was not a law.

No politician except Bryan could believe that a few backwoods members of an Assembly had the right to prevent the children of Tennessee from hearing at school about the theory of evolution. Popular government in America had been allied from the beginning with the people's faith in education. Yet here was an attempt, in the name of majority rule, to destroy the freedom of education on which popular government rested. Bryan insisted that the law was constitutional; but public opinion held that it was a joke. The naive cause of simple majority rule received a set-back.

Western democracy does not give its leaders unlimited power, either for good or for folly. Neither the Executive nor the Representatives, nor both together, have the prerogatives of a Louis XIV or an Elizabeth I. Their task is to apply, and thus to define, and if necessary to amend the constitutional law to which they are subject. In applying the law they have wide latitude; in amending it they can do anything short of preventing their own dismissal—for at that point democracy ends.

Thus the question, 'Who is to have power?', which Plato thought the key to politics, is superseded by the question, 'How is power to be used?' If the Assembly is faithful to the Constitution and has control of the purse, and if the public has not been bewitched by a demagogue, the Executive may think itself the Czar of all the Russias, surrounded by Grand Dukes, and democracy will still prevail.

Friedrich Engels, Marx's right hand, can help us to understand our form of government by his own misunderstanding. 'The State,' he wrote, 'is nothing more than a machine for the oppression of one class by another, and this holds for a democratic republic no less than for a monarchy.' He and Marx had said much the same thing in the *Communist Manifesto* of 1848 when they described the State as 'the executive committee of the ruling class'. Had they written a hundred years later they might have been less confident. For who is 'the ruling class' in Britain today? In Sweden? In the United States?

The once-despised democracy, working through universal suffrage and with constitutional restraints, has made it necessary for all parties to appeal to all groups in the community. The Labour Party in Britain could no more win an election with Trade Union votes alone than could the Conservative Party with the votes of business-men. Classes still exist, in some countries in a vestigial form, but life has become so fluid that no class is strong enough to use the government as its 'executive committee'. This would have startled Marx. It ought to startle the rulers of Soviet Russia. They avoid the discomfort by denying the facts.

Marx would not have denied the facts had he lived to see them. He would have admitted the difference between an oppressive State as he conceived it and a government as we understand it today. The West has outgrown the Marxian

State along with the Marxian capitalism and we are left with a harmless servant, the government—harmless, that is, so long as we watch it distrustfully and are ready to stamp on its toes the moment it shows signs of haughtiness.

The reason why our modern democracies might please Marx and Engels is that we have learned to intervene in economic and social affairs, frustrate the 'inevitable' and insist on something nearer to the heart's desire. The means of our intervention is the government, and a result of our intervention is an increase of the government's influence and power and a proliferation of the government's servants into a vast bureaucracy. This is a danger; but it can be controlled so long as we are dealing with a government which, if we are careful, will remain our humble instrument, rather than with a State which must seek to master us. The difference between the two is democracy.

7

Why did the Russian Revolution fail to produce freedom? If we could answer that question we might learn much about our own problems.

Lenin believed that his new State would be the future model of democracy. It was to be based on the following principles: 'All officials, without exception, elected and subject to recall *at any time*, their salaries reduced to the level of workmen's wages.' This ideal society, Lenin admitted, would have to coerce and even oppress the remnants of the old ruling class. But most of these people would have fled or died, and the rest would not last long. Then complete democracy would reign for the workers and peasants. In time (the date was never specified) the State would wither away.

Lenin may merely have meant that the State as autocrat would disappear, to be replaced by what we have called a government. Yet his ideas of government were strangely innocent, for he wrote that 'the functions of the old "State power" have become so simplified and can be reduced to such simple operations of registration, filing, and checking that they can easily be performed by every literate person, and it will be possible to perform them for "workmen's wages" '.

A charming picture, reminiscent of Thomas Jefferson's dream of an Arcadian America. But Jefferson foresaw an agrarian paradise, whereas Lenin was planning the most rapid industrialisation in history. In any case, political life could never be so simple even on a small Caribbean island.

The will for freedom and democracy was in Lenin's mind and heart. Why, then, was the coercive power of his State not limited to the destruction of the old ruling class? Why, as early as 1921, was the Red Army loosed viciously against the heroes of the October Revolution—the sailors of the fleet at Kronstadt? This was a fatal decision, fatal to Russia's hopes for freedom. Even Soviet heroes were not to be allowed to think for themselves. All forms of deviation quickly became a crime, and the huge slaughter of the Russian people began.

Deviation from what? From the opinions of the Party. And what were the opinions of the Party? The 'correct' interpretation of the sacred text of Marx, and later of Lenin as well. What is a 'correct' interpretation? The interpretation of the men who ruled in the Kremlin this morning.

The great central tragedy of modern history—the subjection of the charming and talented Russian people to a black dictatorship—may be traceable to the fact that Marx thought himself a prophet instead of an economic historian. Prophets don't write books; they announce Revelations. And the sad thing about a Revelation is that it cannot be wrong. When a new man gets control of the Party he may add his own gloss to the divine text. He may even destroy his predecessor for making a false gloss. But the Revelation remains, sacred and final. Thus nobody who obeys the Party can be wrong. Nobody who questions the Party can be tolerated.

The Christian Church had a similar trouble with its own Revelation. So long as only one interpretation prevailed in the West—i.e., the voice of the medieval Church—Christians burned heretics with as smooth a conscience as had the Russians when they put down the revolt in Hungary. John Strachey quotes a Colonel Federor on the latter event. 'Trained by the Communist Party', wrote the Colonel, 'the armed forces of the USSR live up to their international duty. This was demonstrated by the aid they gave to the working people of Hungary....'

The Party was giving aid to the Hungarians by killing them, because the children of the dead would thus be brought up in a perfect Communist society rather than in a Western hell. Colonel Federor may have believed this, for he served a fanatical religion. To him, our politics and our freedom and our democracy are the mark of the devil. To us they are merely inadequate; but at least we have a chance to make them better. Here is the Great Divide: no democrat can be certain that his economic and social philosophy is right; no Communist can imagine that his is wrong.

Yet the Russians are over-ready for democracy: by education, by talent and by the patient wisdom that comes from suffering. The survival of the world may depend upon the Russians attaining their intellectual freedom and admitting in public what millions must think in private, that each man has as much right to his own Marx as he has to his own Bible.

The Christians made an analogous discovery at the end of the Thirty Years War. Gradually, thereafter, the burning stopped.

8

We said that we could control the ever-increasing power of government, if we were careful. This is an act of faith which we must make if we are to have hope for the future. Step by step, as democracy faces the economic and social dangers which Marx believed must destroy it, government has assumed new powers. And it continues to assume new powers every day. We may deplore the tendency but we cannot halt it, short of an unthinkable return toward *laissez-faire*.

We should not fear power in any case, but only the abuse of power. This can be controlled by the institutions we have been developing for two centuries and which we must perfect if we are to save our freedom. We dare not now take refuge in retreat and weakness, denying to our governments the power to master our incessant revolutions in science and technology. Marx warned us that our increasingly sophisticated means of production would destroy our immature political system. If we are to prove him wrong we must not face the mechanical monsters of the space-age with a frugal government which was appropriate to the eighteenth century. Neither must we leave our rulers free to use their necessary powers without our say-so.

'History proves that dictatorships do not grow out of strong and successful governments,' said Franklin Roosevelt, 'but out of weak and helpless ones.... The only sure bulwark of continuing liberty is a government strong enough to protect the interests of the people, and a people strong enough and well enough informed to maintain its sovereign control over its government.' This again assumes the existence of an abstraction called 'the people'. But in real life we have nothing but a mass of 'persons' who tend to form themselves into groups with contradictory interests. No matter how wisely the majority groups may control the government, the remaining groups may be driven to despair and revolt. This was the problem which faced Abraham Lincoln.

The Civil War, Lincoln told Congress in 1861, 'presents the question whether discontented individuals, too few in number to control the administration according to organic laws in any case, can always, upon the pretences made in this case or any other pretences... break up their government.... It forces us to ask: Is there in all republics this inherent and fatal weakness? Must a government, of necessity, be too strong for the liberties of its own people, or too weak to maintain its own existence?'

The question seems unanswerable; but two points may be made on the side of optimism. First, the 'discontented individuals' in Lincoln's case were gathered into one geographical region of a vast federal empire. This made their revolt relatively easy and relatively respectable since it resembled the revolt of the American colonies in 1776. Second, the Civil War became well-nigh inevitable under an administration totally lacking in energy. For four years President Buchanan had let everything drift, under the nihilistic theory that although the South had no right to secede the Administration had no right to interfere. Thus the mere election of Lincoln, who was by no means a nihilist, gave the Southern demagogues their chance. The States of the Deep South had all seceded before Lincoln took office. The Southerners, said the moderate Alexander Stephens, Vice-President of the new Confederacy 'are run mad ... They are wild with passion and frenzy, doing they know not what'.

The tragedy of the American Civil War bears out Franklin Roosevelt's theory that weak governments are more dangerous than strong. Since government must be able to cope, at any moment, with any emergency, and since no one can measure the extent of the next emergency, power cannot in practice be limited although it may be checked and supervised. If the government is incapable of acting, even small crises may drift into disaster. If the government can act without being called to account for its actions, democratic rulers will acquire the habits of despots. The purpose of a constitution, therefore, should not be to limit power but to ensure responsibility and freedom for opposition. Full power to the executive, subject to continuous accountability to an Assembly elected by universal suffrage, such is the ideal for free representative government.

The nearer the approach to universal suffrage, however, the greater the danger of demagogues. Most political problems, as we have said, are institutional. They can be solved, or at least mitigated, by laws and customs which allow the citizens to choose their rulers and compel the rulers to pay heed to the citizens—but not the problem of demagogues. Neither laws nor customs can restrain them. They appeal neither to reason nor to enlightened self-interest, but to passion and prejudice, to the jungle-wickedness at the heart of life which has been revealed by Dostoyevsky in art and by Hitler in action.

'We shall always be stronger than the democracies,' said Hitler, 'in being able to guide their public opinion according to our wish. They cannot defend themselves against such attacks, for otherwise they would have become authoritarian themselves.' We cannot defend ourselves, Hitler thought, because we shall always give the demagogues a hearing. We cannot, by our own faith, silence them until they present a clear and immediate danger. And by that time it may be too late. Their great, astounding lies ('all our troubles are the result of Jews') appeal to every child's belief in magic: Abracadabra and all will be well. Their sadistic solutions ('kill all the Jews and our cause will prosper') appeal to an instinct so dark that we can only indulge it while pretending it is not there.

'They are wild with passion and frenzy, doing they know not what.' Alexander Stephens' words apply to Nazi Germany as well as to the Southern mobs of his own time and of ours. They would seem to apply to a number of 'free' peoples in Africa. We must force ourselves to understand that they could apply to each one of us tomorrow. The best defence against the demagogues is to admit our vulnerability.

If, for example, we allow our globe to become swamped in babies, we shall have carefully, or negligently, bred the causes of countless wars. Over-population and want will create the happy-hunting-ground for demagogues. In the name of nationalism and race-hatred they could settle the population-problem neatly, by having no people. And if we evade this danger, there will be others which we cannot foresee. Each crisis will bring its own demagogues.

All men are susceptible, under certain pressures, to wild orators who promise hope or who multiply despair. When the pinch comes, human suggestibility is the chief enemy of freedom. Almost anybody will believe almost anything if he is persuaded that here lies a simple answer to the perplexing tumult of life. And the 'simple answer' is that the demagogue and his friends should be given control—only for the emergency of course, and always in the name of democracy!

This is not the only folly to which we, as voters, are subject. If want breeds the demagogue and a panic loss of freedom, prosperity breeds sloth and a rejection of responsibility. 'Nothing', says Dostoyevsky's Grand Inquisitor, 'has ever been more insupportable for a man or a human society than freedom.' Public-opinion polls among the American young suggest that the Inquisitor had a disquieting insight. Prosperity, today, is largely administered by the bureaucrats of business, and many young Americans seem to feel that politics could be administered in the same fashion, leaving the boys and girls unencumbered to enjoy the pleasures of abundance. If this means suppressing unpopular opinions and abandoning democracy, they are content. 'You don't hold elections at General Motors', they say, 'and that seems to run smoothly enough.' Again the Grand Inquisitor has the answer: 'In the end they will lay their freedom at our feet and say to us, "make us your slaves, but feed us".'

No one can protect us against these two dangers from within, since no one can force another man to be free. Even if we remain unterrified by threats of poverty and unseduced by wealth, we must still find ways of strengthening our representative systems against the erosion of life. Nothing stands still in politics. Everything improves or decays.

For us, the chief problem is to bolster the power of the trustees, the watch-dogs, the members of Parliament or Congress or whatever assembly. There is a constant tendency for the Executive to slip from the control of the watch-dogs. We can counter this best by making the task of the representatives so clear, so easily understood by the public, so uncluttered by other tasks, that no one is tempted to shirk his duties.

First we must be clear in our own minds that the government is not intended to express the people's will except in the broadest sense. 'The people', let us say, want safety and freedom, and a rising standard of living, and entertainment for their leisure and a certain prestige abroad. They believe that these and other good things can best be secured under democracy. So they want no short-cuts, by way of temporary despots. But if they feel that their government has lost sight of these goals, or is not moving fast enough, they will try another lot at the top. This is as far as the voters can go, by way of being creative. It is not for them to say how these aims are sought, so long as the methods do not sacrifice democracy or freedom.

The Executive should promote the well-being of the community in the broad terms that are mentioned above. The Representatives (especially the Opposition) should make the Executive clearly and constantly responsible for results. Public opinion, or 'the will of the people', only enters in when the results are unsatisfactory, and then only to hand the job to another group. Public opinion is incompetent to attempt the job itself. Thus the need for trustees to keep watch on those who are temporarily in the seats of power.

Quis custodiet custodes? Who will watch the watchmen? In a general sense the voters (with the help of the press) keep an eye on their own representatives—but only in a general sense, for the voters are ignorant of most of the problems of government and bored by some of them, such as foreign affairs between wars. Yet no one else can watch the watchmen; so it must be made as easy a task as possible. This means that the representatives, ideally, should have nothing else to do except watch and question and expose—no access to patronage, no power to influence the budget except by seeking to diminish appropriations, and the minimum of private business for their own constituents. The representatives will thus be forced, in order to look reasonably busy, to promote the public interest by keeping a constant and suspicious eye on the use of power and by passing judgment on all the recommendations of the Executive. If they do not even do that, their dereliction will be easy to detect.

Just as the major problem of power is not 'Who has it?' but 'What are the conditions under which it is exercised?', so the problem of the trustees is 'How simply is the responsibility defined?' Only if it is made very simple can the public be expected to watch the watchmen, can the Assembly become accountable to the voters in the same sense that the Executive is accountable to the Assembly. This is not a question of sharing (and thus diminishing) power, but of sharing control over the exercise of power. This control may sharply diminish the amount of power used, but not the amount of power available for an emergency.

The British Government today shows how executive power tends to encroach upon the function of the representatives. In order to get the programme completed, in each parliamentary session, the Government disciplines its own followers to the point where they have little to do except cast their votes as the Whips tell them—or suffer the consequences of mutiny. The Opposition criticises abundantly, but again with a certain undemocratic discipline. There tends to be a 'party line' in criticism, and he who strays is in danger of losing favour.

No one but the voter can correct this tendency. If an impressive number of voters were to demand more independence for their representatives, the Executive would doubtless yield. But if the voters make no such demand they will find that universal suffrage alone does not ensure democracy. If party discipline becomes absolute, and if such discipline is accepted as the norm, the balance will be upset in favour of the wielders of power and the trustees will be hindered in the discharge of their duties. The major battles thenceforth may take place between colleagues of high cabinet rank, each seeking the top job.

In the United States, where the representatives are supposed to originate legislation as well as to act as watch-dogs, the drift of power toward the White House has been almost uninterrupted from the days of Washington to the days of Lyndon Johnson. This is partly because the Congress has not been a success as a policy-making body, partly because power is by nature the prerogative of the Executive, and partly because the American voter has been given far too much to do and therefore cannot watch his many elected servants and hold them accountable.

In the name of democracy, countless offices which should be appointive have been made elective. The voter may be asked, on a single ballot, to express his choice for fifteen or twenty different jobs. He cannot make an intelligent choice in all cases. And should his candidates be elected he would need more eyes than Argos to keep track of what they did thereafter. So when things go wrong he does not know whom to blame.

A maxim of politics says that if people are given more power than they can wield, that power is in fact taken away from them. Most of the men and women for whom an American votes, on his swollen ballot, have not been chosen by him or by anyone he is ever likely to meet. They have been chosen by a few professionals who in fact make use of the power which the perplexed voter cannot exercise. And if we remember that the voter has to elect state as well as federal officers, and sometimes the local judiciary as well, we shall not wonder if he is swamped by the complications of public life and takes refuge in defensive cynicism.

If the voter elects one or two men, he can hold them sternly accountable for results—including the conduct of the subordinates whom they appoint. But if he elects everybody, nobody is responsible for anything.

9

The British and the American systems, for all their shortcomings, are the archetypes of the two main forms of representative government practised among large nations today. Some of their faults are acquired; these, with experience and good management, may be overcome. Other faults are inherent in human nature; these, if seen candidly, may be guarded against. Future experiments in democracy should take account not only of how these systems do in fact work, but of how they might be improved and adapted to other climes and circumstances.

3
The New Nations

1

MOST of the new nations believe that our forms of democracy are inapplicable to their special cases, and that our tendency to expect others to copy our system is merely another sign of Western provincialism. For the time being this must be expected; but when the first, grievous troubles of these nations have been overcome (for example, when their citizens have enough to eat) man's ancient desire for the freedoms we described earlier will assert itself. Unless Communism or some new forms of government can provide these freedoms, men may look again at the methods of the West.

One of the many unintended results of imperialism is that the world has become a single social-economic system. This is a new phase in human development. It began about 1885 when imperialism was at its most aggressive. The whole globe was soon absorbed into the industrial complex of Western Europe: providing raw materials, labour, and markets for cheap manufactured goods. What imperialism began, the Second World War completed, both in bringing the world ever-closer through technology and in sowing the dragon's teeth of hatred. Our planet has become a small neighbourhood, a polyglot village inhabited by angry strangers. It is against this background that we mention some of the problems in government, and the tentative solutions, involving the new nations.

2

Macaulay denied that any type of government is innately superior. For him, it was all a matter of what worked most conveniently. The environment would determine the forms which were used. If this were true, the new nations of Africa should astonish us with hitherto unimagined systems arising from their hitherto unknown circumstances.

The African tribal groups were given artificial boundaries by their conquerors. Then they cast off their colonial status after only two or three generations during which a tiny minority learned foreign languages and alien systems of government and administration. They are formless, as far as traditional territories are concerned. Their old customs are half-forgotten and their new customs half-learned. They are 'wandering between two worlds, one dead, the other powerless to be born'. And above all they are poor, and suspicious of the West.

Their first aim must be freedom from want. This is one of the collective freedoms. It demands large-scale organisation, so all the more prosperous nations can lend a hand. But we of the West must do so with tact. At the moment (and not surprisingly) we can scarcely say 'Good-morning' politely without being accused of neo-colonialism. But when the problem of poverty in its grossest form has been overcome, what next? The most likely choice is a form of authoritarianism with a one-party government.

Imperialism is still related, for most Africans, to old-fashioned capitalism and to Western democracy. Independence, therefore, tends to be related to 'people's democracies' as in Russia and China. The success of the Soviet Union seems a miracle to those who are seeking to pull themselves up from nowhere. In forty-eight years a country of wooden ploughs and foreign-financed industries has become one of the greatest powers ever seen and has beaten the world at sending a man to take a walk through space.

There is little point, at this stage, in talking to Africans about our much-loved freedoms. What they want is a strong central government with a single party dedicated to rapid modernisation at any cost. This they find in Russia and in China. China has rid Communism of its last taint of Europe and has made it an agrarian, instead of a proletarian, revolutionary force. The fact that China has not solved her agricultural problem is less important than the fact that, starting from nowhere again, she has produced an atom bomb. For some time we shall have to expect, from the underprivileged peoples, an exaggerated praise for anything which seems to put the West in its place.

Sékou Touré, from the former French West Africa, sees the solution for his people in an intensified class struggle which will dispense with every vestige of the past. 'After eighteen months of independence', he writes, 'we are moving into a phase of struggle which is peculiarly difficult since the motives for engaging in revolutionary struggle are less obvious, and actions of sabotage less perceptible. Reaction, dispossessed of the authority which the illegal colonial regime conferred upon it, has put on an impressively "sympathetic" countenance and adopted "friendly" manners, but its destructive intentions are still there.... We must carry on with the mobilisation of the patriotic consciousness of the people.'

This sounds familiar, and it is all the more ominous because we do not know whether there is such a thing as 'patriotic consciousness' in Sékou Touré's country. The Russians are an ancient people, and the Chinese are the most ancient known to history; but the late French West Africa is merely a geographical expression. Unless by lucky chance it has some historical basis for cohesion, it may become a revolution for revolution's sake, on the lines of the Congo. Independence, of itself, does not make a nation.

Aung San of Burma gave the best picture of what makes men feel that they belong together: 'A Nation is a collective applied to a people, irrespective of their ethnic origin, living in close contact with one another, and having common interests and sharing joys and sorrows during such an historic period as to create a sense of oneness. Though race, religion and language are important factors, it is only their traditional desire and will to live in unity through weal and woe that binds a people together, and makes them a nation and their spirit a patriotism.'

This is splendid, but it does not seem to apply to the unhappy subdivisions of once-colonial Africa. People are united across borders (and divided within them) by religion, history, and economic interests. This may explain the appeal of Pan-Africanism. The ex-colonial units are too recently reborn (and in most cases their past is too hopelessly lost and confused) to meet the test of Aung San. But they have one thing in common: the struggle against imperialism. (They also have the legacy of European law, administration, and democratic forms; but these they tend to reject for the time being.)

Of late years we have seen a flood of Pan-African Congresses and Conferences. An African literature has come into being, seeking to make contact with the authentic African culture of the past. Perhaps this will provide a basis for federal union. Perhaps the existing countries will have to rearrange their borders by war or by diplomacy. In any case this is no time to talk to them about the beauties of freedom of speech or freedom of assembly. They will come to that later. People always do, no matter how often or for how long the freedoms are suppressed. At the moment the Africans are in too much of a hurry to wait for argument or to permit opposition. And the great classic freedoms are not made more enticing by the fact that they were born in the West.

3

Throughout this book, in contradiction to Macaulay, we are assuming that an element of choice exists for man and that government is not merely the product of environment. We assume, in fact, that a part of all political power consists in *will* and that no people are fated by hunger or ignorance to become the playthings of a despot. What men think determines how they act. Although the social and economic environment may be largely responsible for what the average man thinks, it is not wholly responsible. And among the leaders—among the men who dream dreams and make revolutions and demand a better future—the area of free will increases. Such men may bring their neighbours to make a rational choice among the forms of government which are practicable at any given time and place. If this be accepted we may ask whether any types of government are *im*practicable for the new nations in Africa? Or do they have a free choice?

At the moment their possible choices would seem to exclude representative democracy. The people do not understand it and the leaders do not want it. They say there is too much work to be done, so they cannot bother with our dilatory methods. They say their people are too uneducated to participate in long-term planning and building: the masses have to be told what to do and made to do it. They say that the cult of personality (the leader-principle), and the constant use of propaganda, are needed for the time being, since dissent means delay and compromise and they have no time for either. They say that at best they have too few trained people to man their governments, so how can they spare any of them to form an unnecessary Opposition?

They say that only a 'people's democracy' can accomplish what the people need, and can be staffed by leaders who know what is good for the people and who are ruthless in pushing ahead and who have no patience for government by gabble. They say that their people prefer a one-party system (all except the small number of Westernised liberals who have to be moved into jail) and that they would be unhappy if compelled to make decisions for themselves. They point out that when 'free elections' were held in the Ivory Coast all the seats were won by Houphouët-Boigny's party; when they were held in Tanganyika, seventy out of seventy-one seats were won by Nyerere's party; and in Senegal all the seats were won by Senghor's party; and in Kwame Nkrumah's constituency in Accra he received 22,780 votes out of 23,122.

Nyerere, who is among the least bitter and the most liberal

of African leaders, insists that parliamentary democracy is impossible in Tanzania today.* He adds, rather naively: 'The notion that democracy requires the existence of an organised Opposition to the Government of the day is false. Democracy requires only freedom for such an Opposition, not the existence of it.' This suggests that Tanzania, unlike any other spot of earth, is blest (or cursed) with inhabitants all of whom think exactly alike—or else that Nyerere, unlike any other man on earth, is so persuasive that nobody can be found to disagree.

Each of the above objections to democracy can be refuted, at least in part. Yet the distrust remains. We must be polite and bide our time, for the motives behind the objections are more solid than the objections themselves. The first motive is the residual hatred of the West because of colonialism. Useless for us to talk about the benefits we have conferred, or to boast of the rule of law. This is the hour of revenge and even the most moderate pleas in mitigation are disregarded.

The second motive is the desire of the 'freedom leaders' to hold on to their jobs. Here we must rid ourselves of the asumption that only white men are corrupted by power. The freedom leaders were for the most part the demagogues, the mob-orators, the born revolutionaries. Such people are usually consumed by the fires of the revolution itself. But in Africa the change came so fast and so peacefully that the Saint-Justs and the Robespierres survived: the Gold Coast became Ghana in 1957, and today the decolonisation is almost complete.† So the revolutionists have out-lived their revolution; but they are fire-eaters by temperament and they do not take kindly to stepping aside for the moderates who might form a democracy. Hence, ironically, they take the

* The union of Tanganyika and Zanzibar became Tanzania in April, 1964.

† We omit South Africa, since in that case the white men and the Bantu arrived at the same time, so the country does not fit into the colonial and ex-colonial pattern.

same line as the imperialists who insist that these people are as yet unfit for self-government. All that any one of them means (and it was all Robespierre meant) is that the mob is unfit to escape from his own tutelage.

Only when they have the vote, and only when they have a free choice of people to elect, can men find means to control their rulers. The American Negro has learned this truth the hard way, and the African Negro will discover it in time. No class, no hero, no political party can be trusted to rule in the interests of the people unless the people, through their representatives, can enforce a daily accounting.

The clamour against 'neo-colonialism' illustrates both these motives for the objections to democracy. Large-scale aid from a western nation, or from rich and powerful private investors, is assumed to have the sinister purpose of establishing outside control. Advice as to how to use the aid is viewed suspiciously and often ignored. This pleases the people who still resent the West and who are more interested in yesterday's grudges than in tomorrow's hopes. It also postpones prosperity, leaving the fire-eater with plenty to complain about and the moderate with not much to offer.

In fact, under a democratic regime there would be no chance for foreign investment to promote a gradual take-over of the country. The United States are an example. The explosion of railway building after the American Civil War attracted British and French capital on a majestic scale. America became the greatest borrowing nation in history. Yet she was not controlled by her creditors. To invent a horror-story, let us suppose that the very rich in Britain, France and the United States had conspired to make the young nation helpless in the hands of international finance. The democratic practice would have spoiled the scheme. Nothing so interesting could take place in the dark, even if the Executive itself had been brought, so long as the trustees (the watch-dogs) were on the job. (The United States got into trouble only when she became the world's greatest creditor. Her trustees did not understand that massive international debts are paid in goods and services and not in petty cash. So her high tariff walls defeated her policy.)

4

We suggested that Nyerere was wrong when he said that an Opposition is not needed for democracy, but only the freedom for an Opposition. However, a highly sophisticated form of representative government, without a formal Opposition, is found in Switzerland. It consists of an executive council which is chosen for a term of three years—the same term as the assembly—and which carries on irrespective of party alignments in the assembly. The council prepares laws for the assembly (a bi-cameral body) and defends them before the assembly. But if the assembly amends them rigorously, or rejects them, the council does not fall. The main parties are represented both on the council and in the assembly. Since the executive cannot be driven from office by a vote of no confidence, and since the executive council and the assembly meet face to face, hostile criticism is often directed toward improving the measure under discussion rather than toward denigrating the majority. (The President, chosen annually by the two houses, acts like the chairman of a committee.)

The Swiss parties agitate forcefully for their ideas in public. Alignments and realignments take place in the assembly as each measure is debated. Any party can call upon the council to prepare and introduce a measure which the party believes should be debated. And the council normally publishes its proposed measures in advance, so that interested parties and adverse criticism may be heard before the final drafting is done. Opposition is free and effective, though not formalised as in Britain.

The members of the council have the right to speak, but not to vote, in both houses of the federal assembly. According to the constitution of 1848 they have not only the duty to introduce bills or resolutions, but also to 'administer the finances of the Confederation, introduce the budget and submit accounts of receipts and expenditures'. Such a system does not need an official Opposition; yet it makes for efficient, businesslike and time-saving conduct of public affairs. Before the introduction of this constitution Swiss politics had been turbulent and sordid.

A similar system was adopted by the island of Barbados. The Barbadian house of assembly received its charter in 1639, and during more than two centuries the small island experienced every form of turmoil to which governments are subject, including the troubles consequent to the abolition of slavery in 1834. In 1876 Great Britain sought to force a confederation upon the West Indies. This led to riots in Barbados but also to the happy invention of the Constitution of 1878 which brought order into the politics of the tiny colony.

The Constitution provided for an executive council of nine members, six of whom were chosen from the assembly. As in Switzerland, the executive council proposed laws and prepared the budget and remained in office for a fixed period, irrespective of the decisions of the assembly. Opposition to a given measure might be strenuous, but it might also be confined to the demerits of the act under consideration since the Government could not be brought down in any case.

Both Switzerland and Barbados have faced problems of unusual severity: four languages and a variety of religions in the one case, racial discords left behind by slavery plus gross over-population in the other. (Barbados has about 1,180 persons per square mile, compared with 550 in Great Britain.) So the efficient and relatively tranquil form of democracy which was first developed in Switzerland might be of interest to new nations, especially in Asia where the hostility to Western ideas is not as inveterate as in Africa.

5

India is the chief reason for a suspension of disbelief in democracy among new nations in Asia. In spite of poverty among the masses, much illiteracy, and a proliferation of babies, and in spite of moral and physical pressure from China, and in spite of a written constitution of 395 articles, India has built and preserved her democracy. Elections are free; opposition parties are free to do their best or worst, though their leaders are sometimes sequestered; the press is free to praise or to revile. All this may constitute a most important political fact. India—as an example—is the best hope for democracy among the underdeveloped nations. No one can say that her resources are not over-strained or that her problems are not seemingly insoluble, yet she does not panic into dictatorship.

Like most of Asia (but unlike Africa) India had never lost touch with her own history and her own civilisation. And unlike Africa she had gained much through her enforced contact with the West. In India the British had time to establish a legal system of independent law courts which gave impartial judgments based upon a law which was not altered to suit the whims of the powerful. And the British promoted schools and universities, and permitted trade unions, and (at intervals) allowed the Congress Party to assume political form and to agitate for independence. So the basic machinery for a democratic system existed in 1947, when freedom was attained. The maintenance of this machinery, sometimes against all hope, is the achievement of the Indians; but the existence of the machinery is to Great Britain's credit.

Nehru was one reason for the survival of democracy in India. Hard pressed, he behaved despotically at times; yet he had the feel of the matter within him. 'Democracy', he wrote, 'is something deeper than a form of government—voting, election, etc. In the ultimate analysis it is a manner of thinking, a manner of action, a manner of behaviour to your neighbour.... In the end you come back not to political terms, but to human terms; or, if you like, spiritual terms.'

India has even experimented in transferring power from central to local agencies. The village councils and the village councillors have a wide influence. This is called 'participating democracy' and it affects remote villages in that huge and over-populated country. It does not solve the problem of controlling power at the centre; but it goes far toward making even illiterate people feel they have a stake in politics.

Gandhi wrote to Nehru: 'I am convinced that if India is to attain true freedom and through India the world also, then sooner or later the fact must be recognised that people will have to live in villages, not in towns, in huts, not in palaces. Crowds of people will never be able to live at peace with each other in towns and palaces.' Nehru did not wholly agree, for he wished to give the blessings of science to his people. He answered Gandhi: 'There is no question of palaces for millions of people. But there seems to be no reason why millions should not have comfortable, up-to-date homes where they can lead a cultured existence. Many of the present over-grown cities have developed evils which are deplorable. Probably we have to discourage this overgrowth and at the same time encourage the village to approximate more the culture of the town.' Here is the hope and the meaning of 'participating democracy'.

Except for India, however, and Malaysia if her life is spared, and the Philippines, the newborn nations of the East seem to have little patience with what the West calls democracy.

In Pakistan a brief period of parliamentary government was followed by a breakdown. President Ayub Kahn has since devised what he calls 'basic democracy', 'something which the people can understand and work'. He described his hopes and plans as follows in the July, 1960, issue of *Foreign Affairs*:

'There are four prerequisites for the success of any democratic system in a country like Pakistan: 1. It should be simple to understand, easy to work and cheap to sustain. 2. It should put to the voter only such questions as he can answer in the light of his own personal knowledge and understanding. 3. It should ensure the effective participation of all citizens in the affairs of the country up to the level of their mental horizon and intellectual calibre. 4. It should be able to produce reasonably strong and stable governments.'

Excellent as this plan may be, it clearly assumes that the citizens are not yet ready to control their government. Later in the same article, Ayub Khan writes: 'I would like to move as fast as possible, but there are many in our country who look askance at this haste. They fear that politicians may return and mess things up once again.' This, however, is one of the purposes of democracy: that politicians should be allowed to return and mess things up. The 'messing up', which so annoys impatient rulers, seems inseparable from free speech, free association, freedom from arbitrary arrest—because one man's 'messing up' may be another man's most passionate hope.

U Thant warned us in 1962 that representative government is not to the taste of many people. 'It is a mistake,' he wrote in *The Times* of London, 'to assume that the political institutions and forms of democracy in most of the newly independent countries will be of the same type as those prevailing in Britain, or that there will necessarily be two main parties competing against each other for the votes of the people.'

So once again we are told that an Opposition is not necessary. Yet we can find no democracy in any country which does not encourage opposition—from the smallest unit of local government to the highest level of policy-making. (The Swiss may have devised an unusually adroit system for criticising and revising and rejecting measures; but it is still opposition.)

With all its faults and dangers, which we have tried to make plain in this book, democracy seems the only form of government which safeguards the freedoms. And without freedom men cannot develop. Until someone finds a better or less awkward form, democracy stands as the only political system fit for man.

6

Is democracy fit only for some men? Or are only a few men fit for it? This we cannot accept. The statement reeks of sanctimony. Either democracy is not the only system for protecting the freedoms, in which case let us find and praise the other ones; or else the freedoms do in fact perish in the absence of democracy, in which case who are we to say that our neighbours are not 'ready' to be free?

The view is widespread that we can separate the sheep from the goats: the potential democrats from those who are doomed to despotic governments. The trouble comes when we try to draw the line. John Strachey, an ardent democrat, wrote: 'All one can really say is that a certain level of general civilisation seems to be necessary in order to enable people to work democratic institutions.' And he adds that when a country is 'overloaded with illiteracy, poverty, racial division' it will not be ready for democracy. India, we have reason to hope, will prove the contrary.

John Stuart Mill made the classic statement in his treatise on representative government. 'It may be laid down as a political truth', he wrote, 'that by irresponsible monarchy rather than by representative government can a multitude of insignificant political units be welded into a people, with common feelings of cohesion, power enough to protect itself against conquest or foreign aggression, and affairs sufficiently various and considerable of its own to occupy worthily and expand to fit proportions the social and political intelligence of the population.'

If one substitutes for 'irresponsible monarchy' some such phrase as 'a civilised and scientifically advanced power', one can see why this passage has long been a favourite defence for imperialism. Africa is the perfect example of 'a multitude of insignificant political units' which need to be 'welded into a people'. Yet imperialism was not a success in Africa. It was not even given time to prepare the people, in its own fashion, for self-government. The people became impatient long before they were 'prepared'. The reason for this impatience may help us to understand why the division of our neighbours into sheep and goats is not only supercilious but unwise.

In the first place, Mill's 'irresponsible monarchy' (whether it be a king or an imperial power) does not in fact spend much time promoting the good of the people. It may do that occasionally, with its left hand; but its own interests are paramount. No irresponsible man, or government, or group will ever strenuously promote the interests of the people because freedom—which is the people's major interest—is a nuisance to the administrator. Thus there was no accumulated goodwill for the imperialists in Africa, which might have delayed the exit of the white man (possibly to the benefit of the Negro).

In the second place, something far more important is happening in the world than the mere 'wind of change' which has been noted in Africa. As a result of the uprooting caused by imperialism and the two World Wars, and of the new scientific revolution which is changing almost every aspect of everyday life, the whole human race is on the move. Most people have always lived on the verge of starvation and hopelessness. They still do; but they now believe it is not necessary. For millennia men endured their horrid fate because there seemed to be no alternative. Now, suddenly, they have become totally impatient, totally intransigent. They will no longer wait for the advice and guidance of their 'superiors'. They intend to 'have a go', on their own, however disastrously.

U Thant was right years ago in saying, 'The world will not live in harmony so long as two-thirds of its inhabitants find difficulty in living at all.' Today he is ten-times right, because the two-thirds have lost all sense of resignation.

The new mood, which extends into the farthest jungles, cannot be changed, but it might be guided. Our fellow men may make mistakes in running their own affairs; but run them they will, even if the final price is slavery for men of their own colour. We can help if we admit that we are all in a similar fix, all trying to find a workable political system. But if we assume that we have already found it, and that they are not even wise enough to look in the right direction, our experience will be rejected and our modest degree of success will be fruitless.

7

The perils of democracy are implicit in history and in human nature. The hopes of democracy lie in our discovery that political institutions can defend us from our weaknesses. We can communicate the discovery if we are humble, though most of the world is not in a mood to hear us today. And we do not always speak ingratiatingly. For instance, if we are ever to catch the ear of the majority we must train ourselves not to shy at the word 'Communism'.

The military aggression of certain Communist states has nothing to do with Marxist theories of democracy or freedom or economics. The aggression is old-fashioned imperialism taking advantage of our present unpopularity. This shocks us inexpressibly since we are on the receiving end. But if we forget the accumulations of bombs and counter-bombs (which are not the subject of this book), and the Russian and Chinese epithets, and the shoes beating on the desks at the United Nations, and if we go back to Marx, Communism is merely an economic system which has not worked very well so far. It was intended to release man for the 'kingdom of freedom'. Some of the new enthusiasts, in Africa or Asia, may discover how to use it for this purpose.

Lenin believed whole-heartedly that his new Russia would be the future model for democracy. It all went wrong; but perhaps it could be started afresh, innocently, by some virgin nation. Divorced from the apocalyptic fanaticism of the Marxists, and from the demonic sadism of Stalin, Communism (not Russian imperialism) might become a decent servant of the people, responsible to the people's watch-dogs like any harassed Executive in the West.

If we are to promote (and protect) democracy we must not assume that every new country which aspires to Communism has been suborned by Russia or China to take part in an obsolescent Cold War. We should help every effort to make Communism and democracy unite. We may learn that the mixture is impossible; but there is no proof yet.

In the end there is the one test. Everything else is machinery; only freedom counts.

Index

Adams, John Quincy (American President), 63
Africa and the Africans, 54, 78–80, 81–2, 89
Alcibiades (Athenian statesman), 14
Alcidamas (Greek statesman), 32
America: see U.S.A.
American Civil War, 48, 69–70
Antigone (Sophocles), 32
Apology, the (Socrates), 13 fn
Aquinas, Thomas: see Thomas Aquinas, Saint
Aristotle, 13, 16–17, 32
Athens, 10–17

Barbados, 85
Barère de Vieuzac, Bertrand, 44, 50
Beria, Laventry, 46
Boer War, 48
Bonaparte, Napoleon: see Napoleon I
Bryan, William Jennings (American lawyer), 64
Buchanan, James (American President), 70

Carthage, 42
Chaeronea, battle of, 17
Challenge of Democracy, The (John Strachey), 28
Chatham, William Pitt, 1st Earl of, 29
Chénier, Marie Joseph, 43
China, 22, 78–9, 86, 92
Christian Church, the, 33, 42, 67–8

Churchill, Winston, 16, 52, 61
Coke, Sir Edward (English jurist), 36
Commager, Henry (American historian), 18, 23
Commonwealth of Oceania, The (James Harrington), 26 fn
Communist Manifesto, The, 65
Cranbourne, Lord (later 3rd Marquess of Salisbury), 57
Crimean War, 48
Critias (Athenian statesman), 14
Crito, the (Socrates), 13 fn

Decline and Fall of the Roman Empire, The (Gibbon), 43
Democritus the Thracian, 10, 32
d'Entrèves, Prof. Alexander, 31
Dostoyevsky, Fyodor, 71

Eden, Sir Anthony (Lord Avon), 60
Elizabeth I (Queen of England), 64
Empedocles, 32
Engels, Friedrich, 65, 66
England, 35–6: see also Great Britain

Federalist, The (essays: Hamilton, Madison and Jay), 26, 52
Federor, Colonel, 8
Fisher, H. A. L. (British historian), 62
Foot, Michael, 60
'Four Freedoms', the (F. D. Roosevelt), 38–9
Frederick William III (King of Prussia), 45

French Revolution, 33, 44, 47
French West Africa, 79
Fuchs, Klaus, 22

Gandhi, Mahatma, 87
George III (King of England), 34
Germany, 62: *see also* Hitler; Prussia
Ghana, 81, 82
Gibbon, Edward (English historian), 42, 43, 48
Great Britain, 48, 52–4, 65, 74, 85: *see also* England
Greece, ancient, 10–17, 19, 31, 34, 42
Grotius, Hugo, 33

Hamilton, Alexander (American statesman), 18
Harding, Warren (American President), 30
Harrington, James, 26
Hayes, Carlton, 44
Hebrew prophets, 31
Hegel, Georg Wilhelm, 43, 45, 46, 48, 50
Hiss, Alger, 22
Historical Evolution of Modern Nationalism, The (Hayes), 44–5
History of the Communist Party of the Soviet Union, The, 47
History of Europe, A (H. A. L. Fisher), 62
Hitler, Adolf, 9, 26, 44, 45, 50, 64, 71
Hobbes, Thomas, 30, 36
Holmes, Oliver Wendell, 21, 30–1, 35, 36
Houphouët-Boigny, Félix (President of Ivory Coast), 81
Hume, David, 52
Hungary, 68

India, 85–7, 89
Institutes (Justinian I), 32

Italy, 18
Ivory Coast, 81

Jackson, Andrew (American President), 25, 63
Jefferson, Thomas (American statesman), 33, 34, 67
Johnson, Andrew (American President), 57
Justinian I (Roman Emperor), 32

Kahn, Ayub, 87–8
Kant, Emmanuel, 37
Khruschev, Nikita, 19, 47
Kinsey reports, 30

Lacedaemonians (Greek history), 14
Law, Andrew Bonar, 48
Lenin, Vladimir, 66–7, 91
Lincoln, Abraham, 69, 70
Lippmann, Walter, 25, 51–2, 64
Locke, John (English philosopher), 34
Louis XIV (King of France), 64

Macaulay, Thomas Babington, 1st Baron, 77
McCarthy, Senator Joseph, 21–3 *passim*
Malaysia, 87
Malenkov, Georgi, 46
Malik, Charles, 19
Mao Tse-tung, 46
Marx, Karl, and Marxism, 56–60, 65–6, 67, 68–9, 91
Marx and Engels, Selected Correspondence of, 58 fn
Melos (Greek island), 15, 42
Mexican War, 48
Mill, John Stuart, 89, 90
Milton, John, 33
Mussolini, Benito, 45

Napoleon I, 44
Napoleon III, 16
Negroes, 83, 90
Nehru, Jawaharlal, 19, 86–7
New Meaning of Treason, The (Rebecca West), 24
New Yorker, the, 61
Nkrumah, Kwame, 81
Nyerere, Julius, 81–2

October Revolution, the (Russian history), 67
Open Society and Its Enemies, The (Karl Popper), 7
Oppenheimer, Robert, 60

Pakistan, 87
Peloponnesian War, 14–15
Pericles, 10, 11, 13, 32
Philip of Macedon, 17
Philippines, the, 87
Plato, 13, 16, 17, 37–8, 65
Pollock, Sir Frederick, 31
Popper, Sir Karl, 7, 58
Pravda, 46
Press, the, 21
Prussia, 45
Puritans, 25

Republic, The (Plato), 13, 37–8
Revolution of 1689, 34
Roman Empire, 42
Roman Empire in the West, General Observations on the Fall of the (Gibbon), 43
Roman Republic, 42
Roosevelt, Franklin D., 20, 24, 27, 38–9, 69, 70
Roussy de Sales, Raoul, 9, 39–40
Rumania, 44
Russia, 46–7, 49, 66–8, 78, 79, 91, 92

Saint-Just, Louis de, 43, 44
Salisbury, Robert Cecil, 3rd Marquess of, 57
Saturday Review, the, 60
Senegal, 81
Senghor, Léopold, 81
Socrates, 10, 12–13, 17
Soong, Dr. T. V., 60
Sophocles, 32
South Africa, 82 fn
Soviet Encyclopaedia, The Large, 46
Soviet history, the *Short Course* on, 46–7
Soviet Union: *see* Russia
Spanish Civil War, 48
Stalin, Joseph, and Stalinism, 21, 22, 45, 46, 50, 91
Stassen, Harold, 60
Stephens, Alexander (American statesman), 70, 71
Stoics and Stoicism, 32
Strachey, John, 28, 36, 55, 89
Switzerland, 54, 84–5, 88

Talleyrand-Périgord, Charles, 23
Tanganyika and Tanzania, 81–2
'Thirty, the' (Greek history), 17
Thirty Years War, 68
Thomas Aquinas, Saint, 33
Thucydides, 11, 13, 14, 15
Touré, Sékou, 79
Toynbee, Arnold, 43, 46

United Nations Organisation, 19, 60, 91
United States of America, 17–30, 34–9, 46, 48, 53, 54–6, 60, 63–4, 69–71, 74–5, 83–4
U.S.S.R.: *see* Russia
U Thant, 88, 90

Washington, George, 54
West, Rebecca, 24
West Indies, 85